BLACK FLORA

DEDICATION

To give honor to God for bringing my parents, James A. Speight, Jr. and Willie Belton Herron, together. From this union they shared a love of this earth and showed me how to appreciate the beauty surrounding us.

Timber Press
Workman Publishing
Hachette Book Group, Inc.
1290 Avenue of the Americas
New York, New York 10104
timberpress.com

Timber Press is an imprint of Workman Publishing, a division of Hachette Book Group, Inc. The Timber Press name and logo are registered trademarks of Hachette Book Group, Inc.

Originally published by BLOOM Imprint in 2022

Printed in China on responsibly sourced paper

Text & jacket design by Hillary Caudle
Endpaper photos by Lauren Crew, with floral styling by Whit McClure

Art on pages 14–15 and 192–193 by Dawn M. Trimble, titled "Stories from the Soil," an original watercolor, gouache, and oil pastel on paper.

Robin Avni, Consulting Designer; Debra Prinzing, Editorial Consultant

The publisher is not responsible for websites (or their content) that are not owned by the publisher.

The Hachette Speakers Bureau provides a wide range of authors for speaking events. To find out more, go to hachettespeakersbureau.com or email hachettespeakers@hbgusa.com.

ISBN 978-1-64326-403-5

A catalog record for this book is available from the Library of Congress.

BLACK FLORA

Inspiring Profiles of Floriculture's

New Vanguard

TERESA J. SPEIGHT

Timber Press · Portland, Oregon

TABLE OF CONTENTS

Black Flora gathers the voices of many of today's most inspiring Black floral entrepreneurs and innovators. Collectively, these floral designers and flower farmers are infusing the profession with a creative force, reflecting a diverse and enriching beauty with their stories.

FOREWORD

Abra Lee

Black people's passion and purpose through the ministry of flowers predates the Civil War in the United States. When the war was over and plantations of the South were burned to the ground and deserted, our formerly enslaved ancestors went back to the ruined gardens. From this land, nurtured by their educated hands, they took cuttings and roots of flowers and planted them in plots around their homes, preserving magnificent heirlooms we still enjoy to this day. This petal-paved past has been the entry point into the world of plants as a viable career for many—including me. My first internship was with a floriculture crew maintaining bloom-filled beds on lavish estates in Atlanta, installations that were so dazzling that the work of our team often brought traffic to a halt. It was here that I first understood what the ancestors understood: the transformative power of flowers.

Years later, flowers would be the epicenter of my first professional milestone. As landscape manager at Hartsfield-Jackson Atlanta International Airport, I was part of a diverse team that included five Black women who installed and maintained a 17-foot floral clock. This is what flowers do; they shape time and take us to places beyond our imaginations. Helping to construct a living timepiece was something I did not think could be exceeded as a pinnacle of achievement. Spoiler alert—it could.

More than a decade after this triumph, a unique new floral challenge presented itself. I was invited by David Hill—associate professor of landscape architecture at my alma mater, Auburn University—to teach a course on Black garden history to his graduate students. While I took the students (called "The Dynamic 9") on a journey

"There is power in flowers, and this book is a recognition of our peers, a new vanguard of floral legends in the making."

of the great gardens and gardeners past, an unexpected gift was delivered to us by the Pennsylvania Horticultural Society: an invitation to participate in their world-renowned plant competition, the Philadelphia Flower Show. Imagine a student team from Alabama showing up in "America's Garden Capital" to contend with the greatest floral and garden designers from around the globe. Tasked to complete a large-scale floral creation for the show's landscape competition, we turned for inspiration to an old friend we had been studying during the semester. The student-led design, entitled "Mixed Shades, Much Joy," was based on the 1941 book *Gladiola Garden* by Effie Lee Newsome, Harlem Renaissance icon and floral heroine. Through the strength of the students' thoughtful design and Newsome's

endearing story, that year we took back home to the South five awards, including a gold medal. It was reaffirmation of what I already knew: Black women and flowers always deliver a winning combination.

It would have been incomprehensible to me, on that floriculture crew many decades ago, that this journey would lead to the highest honor of contributing the foreword for *Black Flora*, written by my friend, mentor, sister, and colleague, Teri Speight. She has curated her chosen floral family and I am honored to be a part of this community. Plants are such an influential and transformational part of our work and world, and many of the artists profiled in Teri's work know each other in real life. Outside of our independent floral achievements we have even achieved victories together. When Talia Boone (of *Postal Petals* notoriety) and I met at the Slow Flowers Symposium, we connected around the idea of having a Black-women-led floral exhibition, created it, and titled it "Music × Flowers." It was hosted by the South Coast Botanic Garden in Palos Verdes, California, a public garden led by Adrienne Lao Nakashima and MaryLynn Mack. Inspired by hip-hop culture in 1990s Los Angeles and the rich legacy of Black Americans in floriculture, it was a floral-filled day at the intersection of rhythm and blooms. Bringing together seven floral artists from the West Coast, the display would have made any of the OG floral and hip-hop legends proud. Who ever thought that floriculture would take us this far?

There is power in flowers, and this book is a recognition of our peers, a new vanguard of floral legends in the making. The colorful profiles in *Black Flora* show how—through the lens of flowers—we shape our future, express our identity, reimagine, and continue to push the floriculture forward as we

always have. Let us join Teri to honor and give these creators their flowers while they are still alive to receive them. We are the past, present, and future. And when it comes to flowers, we are the real deal. We are *Black Flora*!

INTRODUCTION

Teresa J. Speight

My love of flowers developed when I was a child. Growing up in Riggs Park, Washington, DC, my parents always had a garden. Dad planted my mother a rose garden, and we always had bouquets around the house. There was a vase on the dining room table, in each of our bedrooms, and in the kitchen window. Saturday mornings, my parents would create quite the event as we visited our local hardware store, Hechinger's, to buy stick-on decals. We would use those decals to decorate jelly jars and create vases for the roses—I loved the floral decals and always chose those first for my jars.

Our family also observed the summer-time ritual of gardening from seed. We planted marigolds, cockscombs, and portulaca, a ground cover also known as "the sun rose." My mom would gingerly dole out seeds to the three

oldest children to plant however we wanted. (My youngest brother was on her hip, watching, as he was too little.) Giving verbal guidance, she instructed us about spacing the seeds and counting how many to drop in each little hole—she even shared watering advice. Seed-planting was an event we always cherished, as it was the beginning of our lazy summer at home with Mom.

Our front yard was simply beautiful to me. On either side of the front door, a blooming bush stood guard next to plainer green bushes. Dad taught me they were called hydrangea, and their green counterparts were called arbor-vitae. The big blue hydrangea captured my attention. I spent many afternoons gazing at the larger-than-life blooms, dreaming of what kind of vase would be required to enjoy them indoors. If I close my eyes, the memory of each

"Younger generations of Black plant lovers are seeking inspiring examples of successful floral artists and entrepreneurs. When they see their potential through representation of people who look like them in farming and floristry, the possibilities of the future enable their dreams."

floret's crinkles and folds in shades of blue, soft pink, and white comes flooding back.

Dad was my garden hero—I just knew he had magical powers to make things bloom. His seasonal ritual included lugging out the big bag of organic fertilizer from the basement, and I shadowed him as he fed the garden, learning how to pronounce, plant, and care for everything growing in our yard. Dad used *The Wise Garden Encyclopedia* as his reference, and I read that book from cover to cover several times. He was also a designer at the Smithsonian. He helped design a watering system for a chrysanthemum display at the Philadelphia Flower Show. I listened proudly and eagerly as Dad described

his method of tubing and how the water should flow. I have a photo of him amid his chrysanthemum project which hangs in my home office. I knew if he could find joy in creating a watering system for chrysanthemums to be enjoyed indoors, I could listen and figure out a way to enjoy the hydrangea blooms indoors as well. My dad made me proud of his achievements as he encouraged my pursuit of flower gardening. I knew my own garden would provide bouquets to harvest for my house eventually, and I dreamed of watching my own children play in the soil and learning to garden.

While my parents were integral to my love of flowers, there are new Black flower farmers, floral designers, as well as floral creators who are leading the way in today's floriculture industry. And while many of those profiled in this book are not "well known," each has become a floral hero in my world as their talent has evolved and they've stepped into the spotlight. I listen, connect with, and marvel at their remarkable floral narratives as they curate a unique path in an industry where, many times, they are overlooked or ignored. As I navigate my next act, I realized their stories empower me to tap into my creativity while creating unique floral arrangements. The dialogues also encourage me to seek out and curate more conversations about how each person listens to the call of flowers. Each story feeds my imagination as a specialty flower grower and as a floral visionary with a passion for bringing joy to others.

These *Black Flora* stories are quite important. Thanks to my ancestral experiences, passed down through my parents, I always considered myself a gardener. A new appreciation of floral expression as a career has become a part of our culture.

Multiple generations of Black plant lovers are beginning to identify with examples of successful floral artists and entrepreneurs who are culturally familiar. When we are represented by people who look like us in farming and floristry as growers, floral visionaries, and florists, each of us is enabled to imagine the possibilities of success.

I currently create arrangements for private clients and corporate entities. Throughout the season, I receive buckets of random blooms. In each bucket I see a floral story or flower show waiting to evolve. Like a plot in a garden, each seasonal bucket is different. Freshly cutting each stem, removing any foliage that will sit below the waterline, I choose blooms that complement or contrast with each other. Working with each vase provided, I create what I call the "flower show" in my mind. Creating arrangements on a whim presents a challenge from week to week, but it truly brings me joy.

My "someday" flower farm will focus on multigenerational floral education. Educating others is a passion of mine.

LEFT
Teri loves to use whatever is in bloom
from the garden to create floral moments
that capture the season's bounty.

RIGHT
Larger leaves can set the tone in any arrangement.
The structure of smaller, more delicate, blooms
become visible amidst a dark backdrop.

To teach others how to connect with flowers for pleasure—and perhaps as a profession—I knew I needed to learn more about cut-flower farming, so I enrolled in a Floret Flowers Online Workshop to acquire further knowledge that I could share. Simply learning how to grow and arrange flowers can evoke joy. Perhaps I can plant a seed that will encourage others to view horticulture as a career or way of life. As a child, I planted flower seeds in our family's garden. The anticipation as I waited for the seedlings to bloom was exciting. I want to plant seeds of possibilities through the telling of these stories to inspire and empower future Black flower farmers and floral designers.

FAVORITE FLOWER. My favorite plant is *Paeonia lactiflora*, commonly known as the Chinese peony. Like peonies, I consider myself a perennial in the garden of life, always believing in taking my time on the journey to maturity. I am known to have pushed out my leaves to experience life along the way. Now, I am beginning to bloom, and as I unfurl, each petal is different; each experience adds fullness to my life. Like most perennials, I am quiet in my dormancy. When the time is right, I break ground, evolving, unfurling, and fully blooming for a new season. Each spring, as I wait for peony season to arrive in my garden, I am reminded to bloom fully before it is too late.

"With ancestral sharecropping roots, connecting with the Earth is authentic to me. My ancestors' hands have helped build and feed our family for generations. To not honor this Earth would disrespect my heritage. I am passionate about sharing the stories of Black voices in the green world."

ASHLEY ROBINSON

Botanical Artist

LOS ANGELES, CALIFORNIA

12AMSUNSHINE

Fashion meets flora in the hands of Ashley Robinson, who creates and photographs botanical couture. She named her floral studio 12amsunshine, a nod to her maternal grandmother Thelma Anderson and her 1980s DJ persona, Midnight Sunshine. The name totally fits Ashley's personality and joyful floral art.

"Having an outlook where I can dwell in a place of purpose, peace, and spirituality allows me to create what I imagine in my mind's eye."

GROWING UP, Ashley and her sister were fans of anything fashion-related, often cutting up copies of Vogue to create collages of outfits they dreamed of wearing. She studied strategic advertising at Virginia Commonwealth University, graduating in 2015 and moving to Oakland, and then later, to Los Angeles. An interest in consumer psychology and trend research, born from that same early interest in recreating outfits from magazine photos and advertisements, landed her work as a social media manager and strategist.

As she sketches design ideas, now inspired not by fashion magazines but the flora of Southern California, Ashley seeks out the right botanicals to use, constructs the piece, models it, and then photographs the completed outfit.

The results are exquisite and fascinating, from layers of red eucalyptus leaves embellishing a fitted bodice to deconstructed spider mum petals transformed into a lacy choker, to shiny tropical foliage elevated into a verdant bustier, or even 200 individual

ABOVE
Each gathered element has a role to play in the final production. Ashley allows the gathered materials to guide her vision throughout the process.

OPPOSITE
Gathered elements for a "camouflage" bomber jacket featuring varieties of moss.

OPPOSITE
Botanical photography with
Ashley's favorite gloriosa lilies
and sprigs of allium.

delphinium florets cloaking an off-the-shoulder top.

The process allows Ashley to be her own muse, bringing ideas to life and sharing them via social media and her website, 12amsunshine.com. "It feels great knowing I can help people find a new way of looking at flowers and nature," she says.

"Since I was a teenager, the only thing I've loved to photograph was Mother Nature herself—flowers were always my favorite. I've discovered my creative calling and a new form of expression through botanical couture. My gifts aren't a particular skill, they lie in the embodiment of my unique wholeness."

A childhood of hiking and camping, as well as living in Italy with her military family, gave Ashley a greater awareness of nature and the environment. When she was nine, the family settled in Virginia, where her mother planted a garden filled with flowers, vegetables, and herbs. As a teenager, Ashley began to photograph the garden, taking her first portraits of a rose her mom planted. "The intricacy of each petal was amazing, and my mother lavished all of her attention on her rose," she remembers. Ashley turned the photograph into a Mother's Day card "to thank my mother for instilling in me a love and appreciation for flowers."

Ashley's botanical couture brings together her childhood love for nature with a modern aesthetic vision. "It used to be all about the bloom; however, I realize the bloom would not exist without the plant. I appreciate all aspects now—from the roots to the leaves—and, of course, the blooms. All of these features can be incorporated into wearable botanical accessories."

In recent years, she began searching for other African Americans in the floral industry who looked like her, while also drawing from "divine remembrance" as an ancestral reference in her own craft. "Flowers helped me define my creative path. When I designed a top out of palm leaves purchased from the flower market, I knew this was going to be my calling," she says. "There's a joy I experience when I create wearable botanical art."

FAVORITE FLOWER. Ashley is led by mood and color when she thinks about flowers, and she sees the potential in each bloom and blossom. "Right now, my favorite flower is the gloriosa lily. It is whimsical in form and the colors are super vibrant."

OPPOSITE, CLOCKWISE FROM TOP LEFT
Ashley designed this Mother's Day arrangement featuring oncidium orchids, roses, carnations, anthurium, and assorted greenery.

Raw materials for an artichoke bracelet.

Ashley models her celosia drop earrings.

A single yellow tulip. "I was drawn to the shape of the stem and leaves."

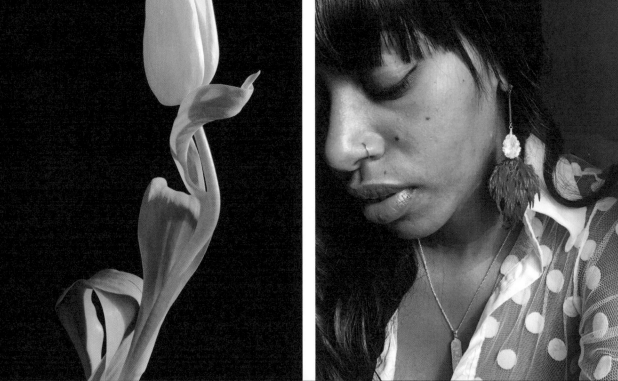

GINA LETT SHREWSBERRY

Floral Designer

SACRAMENTO, CALIFORNIA

INSPIRATIONS BY GINA,
FLORAL AND EVENT DESIGN

Gina Lett Shrewsberry is the owner of Inspirations by Gina, a Black-owned floral and event design boutique that creates a couture floral experience to tantalize the eyes and transform the soul. Loving color, Gina and her team draw inspiration from ethnic fabrics and find accents from local and global artisans. When they design an event, it is always distinctive, expressing each client's personality and desires. Inspirations by Gina is the only Black florist on San Francisco City Hall's preferred vendor list.

A CALIFORNIA NATIVE who graduated from the University of San Francisco, Gina Lett Shrewsberry spent years as a corporate banking officer. She enjoyed the creativity of producing company events, not realizing her skill set in this area was laying the groundwork for a future as a wedding and event planner and floral designer.

It was not until Gina spent extended time with her mother, as her care-taker, when she first learned of her mother's past as a farmer. Raised in Vallejo, California, Gina grew up in a middle-class African American neigh-borhood where gardens were filled with fruit trees, vegetables, and, of course, beautiful roses—and where people took pride in their yards. These conversations with her mother created a stir within her, making her more curi-ous about growing plants and working with the land. "My husband encour-aged me to walk away from a career in finance to further explore my love for creating events." In 2008, she launched Inspirations by Gina, focusing on wed-ding and event design.

ABOVE
A charming Inspirations by Gina arrangement features foliage and flowers from Park Winters, a historic boutique inn and private event venue in Winters, California, and roses sourced from a Sonoma County farmer.

OPPOSITE
Flowers for this arrangement were hand-picked from the grounds at Park Winters, where Gina often provides clients' wedding florals. "The table is a family heirloom my grandmother had more than 100 years ago," she says. "It ties back to the legacy of my mom, aunt, and grandmother."

"I learned these words from the Signature CEO Conference: 'Think like a small business and you will always be a small business. Don't think small. Instead, always think about how you can improve yourself, your business, and your community.'"

As her business grew, Gina noticed brides often thought about flowers last. "There were many times the DIY brides would not have their wedding florals assembled prior to the day of the wedding. I often stepped in to assist. It became such a regular occurrence, I added floral design in my services for a fee."

A florist friend saw Gina's arrangements and recognized her natural ability to capture beautiful combinations. She suggested Gina refine her techniques at a local community college. "I paid $98 each semester for three semesters of classes to enhance my floral skills, and that has been worth every penny," she laughs. Gina began by creating floral arrangements for Sunday services at her church, encouraged further when her pastor commented that she had "God-given talent" as she admired her work.

By October 2019, Gina took the leap to focus her boutique studio solely on floral design. Her signature style is elegant, romantic, and serene with a nod to Mother Nature.

Like many florists, she had to get creative during the past few years to diversify beyond weddings and events. Inspired to adapt, her studio now offers a new delivery service to local clients and supports flower farms throughout Northern California with flower subscriptions and designer's choice arrangements.

"It has been a great way to see exactly how flowers impact people in a positive way," she says. "It's just amazing to create a bouquet to be delivered from one friend to another and then see the joy on the face of the recipient."

As the conversation about race in this country continues, Gina notes how many African Americans in floriculture have hesitated to attach their persona or likeness to their businesses. "The fear this would cause a decrease in our businesses and followers is a scary thought, but I have made a conscientious decision that I do not want to hide anymore. I am standing on the shoulders of other African Americans who paved the way for me to be in this industry," she says. "I want to make another little brown girl know I am creating something for her to be proud about. I also want to pass on the legacy to my son, so he also knows it is never too late to start a new career."

Foraged, native-plant material mixed with elegant cultivated
roses offers a unique option for use in arrangements.

A circular arch caressed by an abundance of soft
colored flowers—such as roses, dahlias, lisianthus,
and more—anchor this borrowed view.

Gina continues to bloom, with guest spots on several podcasts and a Black Florists Award nomination in 2022. In 2022, she was also proud to be the first African American floral designer in the thirty-eight-year history of the Bouquets to Art Exhibit at de Young Museum in San Francisco, CA. Gina is also a sought-after speaker, after being featured at The Great Grow Along, The San Francisco Bay Flower & Garden Show, *The Sustainability Podcast*, *Mornings with Mayesh*, and The Slow Flowers Summit.

FAVORITE FLOWER. My favorite flower is sea holly (eryngium). It is stately, spiky, and has a steely blue color that is one of a kind. I also love hydrangeas, dahlias, and garden roses, all of which make a memorable statement in any arrangement or at any event. Each of these flowers reflects my personality.

SHANDA ZELAYA

Floral Designer

MARSHALL, VIRGINIA

FLOR DE CASA DESIGNS

Flor de Casa Designs is a Virginia-based floral design studio specializing in weddings and events for clients in the greater Washington, DC, metro area. Owner Shanda Zelaya cares deeply about the environment and she expresses these values through artful, foam-free arrangements with botanicals sourced from local flower farms.

FLOR DE CASA means "House of Flowers" in Spanish, the language Shanda Zelaya spoke while growing up in Costa Rica, surrounded by botanical beauty and lush greenery.

Her family immigrated to America and settled in New York when she was nine. Shanda loved when her mother asked her to arrange flowers purchased at the supermarket for a party or meal.

"The blooms of my mother's hibiscus bush always fascinated me," she recalls. "Even as a teenager, flowers were a bit of a hobby." But the idea of a career as a floral designer never occurred to her. At this stage, she bypassed college, working as a medical interpreter and in software marketing.

When planning her own wedding in 2015, Shanda spent $700 on bulk flowers and bunches from the supermarket. "I knew what I wanted and there was only one way to make it happen," she confides. Her idea was to cluster vases varying in sizes at the center of each

OPPOSITE

Shanda designed this tablescape for a micro wedding of only fifteen guests. "The couple wanted to incorporate vibrant colors using tropical blooms to pay homage to the groom (who is from Costa Rica) and his home country," she says. "They wanted to create an upscale, intimate event that was relaxing enough for their guests to simply enjoy the evening and have fun."

"My flower journey has taught me how, in the same way food nourishes our body, flowers nourish our soul."

guest table for a lavish look that transported her to her Costa Rican roots.

On their first anniversary, Shanda and her husband stayed at a charming bed and breakfast. The innkeeper asked to see their wedding photographs and admired the flowers. When Shanda explained she had designed her own wedding florals, the woman assumed she was a professional florist. The experience reinforced Shanda's latent dream of working with flowers and being an entrepreneur.

"That was like the little light bulb in my head and it made me ask, 'Why don't I?,'" she recalls. "I was really good at selling in the technology sector, but it wasn't for me. I was not built to work in a full-time capacity in an office."

Acting on advice from a makeup artist friend who worked in the wedding industry, Shanda launched a simple website and marketed Flor de Casa Designs on a service-based app called Thumbtack. She took close-up photographs of blooming plants while on neighborhood walks and purchased other flowers to make bouquets and boutonnieres, which she convinced friends and her husband to model for more photographs. "It was the only way I could think of to show my work, so other people could see what I was capable of and trust me enough to design their wedding," she says. Her strategy began to pay off. "I booked my first client within a month and after that I had a wedding pretty much every single month."

Today, Flor de Casa Designs serves wedding and event clients from Shanda's home-based studio, recently relocated to Marshall, Virginia, which is closer to the local flower farms where she shops. "A lot of our events happen in Virginia's wine country, but they can also be in a chic DC-area hotel," she explains. "I serve couples who have different looks and aesthetics, which keeps my designs looking a little different. My couples are seeking something beyond what they would consider traditional, and personally, I'm attracted to a looser, airy, organic floral style."

Shanda's journey to flowers has led to collaborations with home goods retailers such as West Elm. In 2020, she was named to the "Top 10 Florists" list in Washington, DC, by the website Wedding Rule, and also highlighted as one of the 50 Best Florists by actress Drew Barrymore in *Drew*, her new magazine. Shanda is happiest when designing for the pure joy of being creative.

"Designing for me is an art form and I believe you need to dedicate time to your chosen art form. You need to love your flowers. You need to relish the joy of making something beautiful."

FAVORITE FLOWER. As a florist, Shanda sees beauty in every flower and loves each one equally. Yet, she says her favorite go-to flower is the ranunculus, loved for its dainty blooms, delicate petals, and variety of colors. "They can create an understated, yet luxurious arrangement—and understated luxury is Flor de Casa's signature attribute."

KRISTEN GRIFFITH-VANDERYACHT

Floral Designer	SEATTLE, WASHINGTON
	WILD BLOOM

Floral artist Kristen Griffith-VanderYacht is the founder and creative director of Wild Bloom, a wedding and event studio specializing in artfully crafted floral arrangements celebrating nature. In Kristen's hands, each floral piece expresses the unpredictable, ever-changing spirit of the wild. In 2020, he burst onto the small screen as the charismatic head judge and mentor of Netflix's *The Big Flower Fight*, instantly capturing the hearts of flower lovers around the world.

ABOVE
A wedding bouquet for a bride who requested all-white flowers with no foliage. "Since I like a challenge, I said, 'Yes,' but only on one condition," Kristen explains. "I get to choose the flowers. These gorgeous orchids felt like the perfect blend of classic and modern forms."

OPPOSITE
A beautiful pairing of spring-blooming hellebores and flowering mimosa branches in a low compote illustrates Kristen's playful design aesthetic.

THROUGH WILD BLOOM, his Seattle-based studio, Kristen Griffith-VanderYacht designs luxurious florals for weddings and events. He started his floristry career a decade ago, crediting his interest as a child to flowers and gardening. "Although I am self-taught, my work reflects my aesthetic flair as I add distinctive twists to any arrangement I create," says a confident Kristen. "I truly believe art is an expression of the designer, of the maker."

In 2020, Kristen's intersection of experiences—including flowers, professional theater, and graduate studies in psychology—collided as he was named head judge on Netflix's *The Big Flower Fight*. "Being on *The Big Flower Fight* was one of the most incredible experiences of my life," he notes. "You often hear about the horrors of working in the television industry. The dramatic divas, the cold-hearted producers, and the self-absorbed cast members. This experience was nothing like that. What was even more special is that my family was able to come to the set a few times. What stood out to me most was how aware I was of my position as a gay Black man on what was going to be a big show on an even bigger network. I had never seen anyone who looked or spoke like me on a television show like this one before. I knew what was at stake, not just for me but for little brown boys everywhere."

One of the lessons Kristen learned from his mother while growing up in Detroit was to always do more than just show up. Encountering different experiences in life, he realized it was up to him to recognize his self-worth, his talent and, most importantly, that he mattered. Kristen's upbringing shows in his taste for the finer things in life. With two siblings vying for Mom's attention, Kristen quickly realized the garden was the best place to enjoy quality alone-time with his mom. From a young age, he gained knowledge about selecting, planting, and maintaining beautiful flowers and plants.

As he continues to expand his presence in the world of floriculture as a show host, events specialist, social media personality, and more, Kristen encourages others to use flowers as a medium to work through doubts and fears. "If I can just connect the dots for others in communities everywhere to realize the power of flowers and how they can help heal, the world would be a better place," he says.

Theater was another place Kristen felt at home and while attending Boston Conservatory, a performing arts college, he was cast in the national tour of *Rent*. "Theatre, for me, was always about connecting with people and making a difference in someone's life through a performance," he says in retrospect.

After the *Rent* tour concluded, Kristen stayed in New York and enrolled in Columbia University's graduate psychology program. He intended to become a school counselor but found himself dreaming about flowers, wandering through neighborhood flower shops and New York's flower district.

In 2011, he landed an internship with Sprout Home in Brooklyn's Williamsburg neighborhood and

LEFT
A romantic arrangement with Cafe au Lait dahlias, blush-toned roses, and fluffy smoke tree blooms. According to Kristen, "I have always been drawn to the unconventional type. The outlier. The overlooked. It's the same in design, I fight against the pressure to color inside the lines."

RIGHT
Kristen's breathtaking installation uses spring-flowering branches to set a scene for a boudoir session, photographed at the Rainier Chapter House in Seattle.

"Flowers have always been a part of my life. It just took me twenty years to see. They have been there in the background playing a role in every monumental moment."

soaked up all he could learn from the head designer Doan Ly. Yet the experience also taught Kristen that he needed to listen to his own artistic muse. When he later opened his first floral business, called Full Aperture Floral, Kristen knew getting published was one of the best (and most afford-able) ways to market his work. He recalls naively arriving at a magazine photo shoot in New York holding a huge floral arrangement and attract-ing the photographer's attention. "He gave me a seat at the table," Kristen recalls. "I have been quite fortunate to have opportunities shared with me. Sometimes when I show up, I can tell that my race splinters my identity. There are clients who are not quite sure how to take me as an openly gay, African American man. It's like having two entrées on the same plate. Instead of working to bend myself to please another person's impression of me, over time I have learned believing in myself and my talents is the best way to be authentic and find balance."

FAVORITE FLOWER. Kristen's favorite flower is the hellebore, specifically the sultry Black Onyx and Blue Diamond cultivars, which have dramatic, dark burgundy hues.

OPPOSITE
Kristen's autumn-inspired "designer's choice" arrangement in a coffee-and-cream palette. The centerpiece features apricot lisianthus, white flannel flower, merlot fall foliage, and ornamental feather grass.

HERMON BLACK

Floral Designer

ARLINGTON, VIRGINIA

HB FIORI FLORAL STUDIO

HB Fiori is a home-based floral studio recognized for creating classic arrangements with a wild, unstructured twist. Floral designer Hermon Black believes flowers bring beauty, grace, and harmony into the home, and she customizes every arrangement using distinctive, premium botanicals grown locally and on US farms.

HERMON BLACK ESTABLISHED HB Fiori Floral Studio in 2015, drawing from a childhood love of floral arranging while growing up in Addis Ababa, Ethiopia, her interior design studies when she came to the United States as a college student, and a career managing a fine jewelry retail department.

She serves private and corporate clients in the Arlington community and the surrounding DC metro area, specializing in intimate parties, events, and everyday arrangements. Hermon originally wanted to source the same outlets where professional florists shopped, gaining access to high-quality blooms at wholesale prices.

"When I started designing flowers, my thought was to train my friends and neighbors to know they needed to have gorgeous flowers in their homes on a regular basis," she recalls.

The HB Fiori aesthetic draws from Hermon's memories of being surrounded by a proliferation of native African flora in her backyard. Her parents encouraged their daughter in

gaining the proper skills to beautify the home—including decorating with flowers. Even at the age of seven, Hermon listened to the stories shared by her mother's friends of how they adorned their homes, including which flowers were used in centerpieces and how the tables were set.

"It was a very special act of bonding when my mother gave me access to her vast collection of cherished crystal vases," she recalls. "She would tell me how they could be used for specific arrangements. I loved to choose different sizes and shapes of vases, based on the size, shape, and color of the flowers and greenery I foraged, which allowed me to experiment, heeding my mother's expertise and advice."

After attending Addis Ababa University and studying history, her dream of coming to the United States became a reality. Hermon imagined herself studying interior design in the United States because there was no interior design curriculum offered in Addis Ababa. "The plan was to return after my education in the United States

"Flowers can transport you to a harmonious existence. Having flower arrangements nearby creates a sense of peace and calm no matter where you are. I find peace as I arrange florals and again when I deliver my bouquets. Seeing the smiling faces of each recipient makes me happy."

and join my Dad, ensuring his engineering firm would add interior design services," she says.

In 1997, at age twenty-two, with her student visa and green card in hand, Hermon landed in San Francisco, but soon moved to Rochester, New York, where she attended college to study art and interior design. By then, returning to Ethiopia was not safe, and her family encouraged her to remain in the United States. While working in retail management, she began to dream of starting a business that would be compatible with raising children.

As Hermon noticed how friends from all over the world celebrated daily

occurrences, "I began to offer my services as a floral designer and was pleased at the positive response," she says. "People appreciate quality fresh floral arrangements in their homes, especially unique arrangements." Visiting area farms to pick up flower orders, creating arrangements, and then delivering them has proved therapeutic not just for her customers, but for Hermon, as well. She believes flowers are an international language. "When I create with flowers, it is a way to show grace and gratitude to nature, without saying a word."

With the success of HB Fiori, Hermon projects a quiet confidence in her talent, aware of the incredible value

she offers design clients. "I have had to develop a thicker skin and learn to hide how uncomfortable it has often been to not be taken seriously or have my talents undervalued or too unrecognized," Hermon says. "As an African woman, I always go above and beyond to prove my talent is real. Many people do not realize flowers are at the center of everyday celebrations in Africa. We do not consider flowers to be a luxury—a necessary luxury conveying our gratitude to the wonders of nature. Flowers are a part of everyday life."

FAVORITE FLOWER. Hermon says choosing a favorite flower is like choosing your favorite child, which she could never do. "Lately, a viburnum with vivid red berries caught my eye and I was able to use one or two branches in an arrangement. I guess you could say I have favorites of the moment."

OPPOSITE
Hermon designed this dreamy butter cream-hued centerpiece with roses, dahlias, zinnias, and butterfly ranunculus for Beyond the Blackout, a District of Columbia event co-produced by LaJoy Plans and Bright Occasions in response to the larger Black Lives Movement and inequities in the events industry.

THE WILD MOTHER

Floral Activists

The Wild Mother Creative Studio is a multidisciplinary art studio owned by Afro-Indigenous sisters Lauren Palmer and Leah Palmer. The studio is based in the heart of the downtown Oklahoma City Arts District on Kickapoo, Osage, Wichita, and Comanche land. Lauren and Leah are joined by fellow designer and younger sister Callie Palmer, sharing their love for and honor of culture, storytelling, and an affinity for natural elements and color theory in floral art.

LEAH AND LAUREN PALMER established The Wild Mother Creative Studio in 2013 as a means to create generational wealth and to express their belief that "Art is Medicine." "We know a greater value is shared through wisdom, language, a connection to the Divine, a relationship to the land, stories, and truth," Lauren explains. With their younger sister Callie, the siblings acknowledge their roots while exploring the ways their business and creative endeavors are directly linked to guidance from ancestors' stories and wisdom from their elders.

The Wild Mother's offerings include floral design for large-scale events and weddings and seasonal arrangements offered at holidays. Their aesthetic process is outlined in "The Eleven Reasons Flowers Matter in the Landscape of Your Life," penned in 2015. The narrative begins with "story"

OPPOSITE
A charming spring garden
arrangement designed from
the hands and imagination of
The Wild Mother studio.

ABOVE
Ebullient and vibrant florals reflect
The Wild Mother's aesthetic.

PREVIOUS
In May 2021, #sendflowerstogreenwood was led by
The Wild Mother Creative Studio with the assistance
of nearly thirty floral artists, who created "The
Covering," a floral-filled space of meditation
and reflection to commemorate the Tulsa Race
Massacre of 1921, one hundred years earlier.

*"Our flowers are more than just a decoration;
they are a mouthpiece, a narrator, a storyteller."*

and "life" and continues through the principles of design, the sensory and memory-inducing character of flowers, as well as nostalgia and tradition. This approach is reflected in their studio motto: "More than Flowers." "Our flowers are more than just a decoration; they are a mouthpiece, a narrator, a storyteller," Lauren and Leah write on The Wild Mother's website. The sisters share one voice as young creative artists mindfully and intentionally navigating a marketplace where Black and Indigenous art is rare.

Growing up, it was important for the Palmer sisters to preserve and connect with lessons from their heritage, as they embraced elders' stories told from Black church pews, whispered in red Oklahoma clay, hard-earned in Mexican kitchens, and passed from Choctaw blood memory. Gathered lessons of identity guided the sisters like a North

Star, especially while being raised in a mostly white evangelical community. The knowledge that their ancestors tended the land while in bondage is directly linked to the sisters' practice of tending to nature's gifts in freedom.

The early conversations about their creative studio began on the Shawnee, Oklahoma, campus of Oklahoma Baptist University, which Lauren and Leah attended as undergraduates. Having studied music theory and piano since she was a toddler, Lauren completed her degree in 2013 with a multidisciplinary BA in music and anthropology. "I began what I now know as a practice of reconnection—to cultural ways, to language, to song, to ancestors, and their rhythms," she says. "For me, this meant unlearning my habit of making myself palatable for others' tastes and instead allowing the richness of all I carry, all I am, to be un-stifled as I celebrate the beauty of my birthright." Leah studied literature and graduated with a BA in English, followed by a MA in English, which she earned in 2015.

The sisters were raised among very few Black and Brown people in largely white homogenous spaces—where members of the community reflected one another politically, religiously, ethnically, and otherwise. College life was a natural time for them to explore their own beliefs, but also became a place of profound transformation as they learned who and what spaces honored their identities. For Leah, a driving motivator for founding The Wild Mother Creative Studio was to create a world in which her identity, relationship to land, and exploration of ancestral wisdom would be prioritized and protected.

At the time Lauren and Leah began The Wild Mother concept, Callie was a young high schooler, overhearing her older sisters' conversations about business, identity, and creativity. Her current role as the studio's fellow designer

developed more recently. "As our business evolved, revealing who we are became part of a bigger discussion. We were initially cautious about expressing our ethnicity in our online presence for fear it would jeopardize our ability to make money," Callie says. At first, the studio took a "let the art speak for itself" approach, but things shifted dramatically in the summer of 2020.

In the wake of international unrest after the murders of Ahmaud Arbery, George Floyd, and Breonna Taylor, the sisters made a conscious decision to be fully transparent about their identities—no longer minimizing, silencing, or attempting to be palatable. They realized this allowed them to lead from a place few others can. They began their leadership as art activists in the floral industry posting a graphic to Instagram saying, "Black Women Created This," in solidarity with the anti-racist movement and as a challenge to their peers to acknowledge the Black story of America, fraught with pain and beauty. "We felt liberated for once," Leah recalls. "The freedom of showing up in this community has been healing."

Flowers for an intimate wedding set
the stage. A communal table at a
micro wedding is a wonderful way
for couples to celebrate the love
they share with the closest ones
in their lives, says The Wild Mother.
"The beautiful thing is that you
don't need to sacrifice your wedding
vision or the quality of your details."

An inviting corner at The Wild
Mother studio, where a vintage
galvanized sink is deep enough
for filling flower buckets.

"Nature is nurturing and beautiful and soft and welcoming—and at the same time, it can be terrifying and intense. We hold those tensions … in every arrangement."

Their studio's name "reflects the paradox and tension that we see in the natural world and in the Divine," Leah continues. "Nature is nurturing and beautiful and soft and welcoming—and at the same time, it can be terrifying and intense. Early on, when we were exploring our design aesthetic as florists, we talked about holding those tensions, while making sure that in every arrangement there is something beautiful and welcoming, but with a jagged edge or texture next to it."

The women's art-activism calls attention to broken communities while creating spaces for reflection and honor. From this belief came an annual project called "Send Flowers to: Requiem and Response Through Floral Outpourings," which encourages other artisans and florists to be more mindful and intentional through their creativity.

In May 2021, The Wild Mother curated a floral installation to pay homage to the survivors of the 1921 Greenwood Massacre in Tulsa. Working with a team of nearly thirty volunteer florists, they completed stunning, site-specific installations, as well as floral arrangements dedicated to the Greenwood community, while sharing a story which had remained largely hidden for almost a century about a racist white mob's attack on a thriving Black town in Tulsa, killing three hundred men, women, and children. Their "Send Flowers To" project was emotionally heavy, yet a beautiful way to honor a broken community with flowers.

FAVORITE FLOWER.

Lauren: Champagne rose
Leah: Tweedia
Callie: Hellebores

MIMO DAVIS

Flower Farmer

ST. LOUIS, MISSOURI

URBAN BUDS

Karen "Mimo" Davis is a farmer-florist and co-owner of Urban Buds: City Grown Flowers with her friend and business partner, Miranda Duschack. Urban Buds produces flowers year-round and grows eighty-plus varieties annually. The farm sells wholesale to St. Louis-area florists, provides wedding and event design services, and brings flowers to the weekly Tower Grove Farmers' Market.

TRULY AN URBAN agriculture pioneer, Mimo Davis believes flowers are a form of social work, bringing joy and fulfillment to others. As a partner in Urban Buds: City Grown Flowers, Mimo grows blooms in the heart of her community in Dutchtown, a neighborhood in south St. Louis.

There, she exposes farming to those who may not otherwise have an opportunity to connect with nature. Mimo also shares her expertise with other flower farmers as a mentor and educator in the cut-flower industry and through her position as Vice President on the Board of Directors for the Association of Specialty Cut Flower Growers.

Mimo's introduction to the horticulture and floricultural industries was unexpected. In 1989, while she was living in New York City, Mimo flew to Missouri to attend her mother's wedding. The newlyweds asked Mimo to house-sit while they were on honeymoon, a task that required caring for her mother's greenhouse and yard, both packed with flowers. Mimo knew nothing about plants but was determined to keep them alive. She spent the week visiting local garden centers, carrying a leaf from each of her mother's plants to make a scrapbook of care information, grateful for tips shared by nursery staff. During her week-long stay in Missouri, Mimo fell in love with flowers as she became fascinated with everything growing in her mother's alluring greenhouse.

"I had a nonprofit program administrator position in New York City, working for Covenant House, an organization serving homeless youth. It was a high heels and dress-for-success kind of deal," Mimo explains. "I was living in a studio apartment, paying $1500 a month in rent. And I came out to Missouri for the wedding and realized, wow, I could have a twenty-acre farm here for what I'm paying in rent. I was ready to retool myself. I wanted a different life."

Within six months, Mimo's new passion for flowers inspired her to leave her social work career and relocate from New York City to a farm she purchased in Ashland, Missouri. She

attended Lincoln University to study horticulture and started Wild Thang Farm. "I built up this business, growing flowers on about five acres, with five employees," she continues.

After thirteen years of growing and selling cut flowers, Mimo stepped away from the farm to pursue another degree. She earned a master's degree in Plant Soil Science and Horticulture at North Carolina Agricultural & Technical University, in Greensboro, North Carolina. In 2008 after graduation, she returned to Missouri and

joined the Cooperative Extension Service, which blended her original social work training with horticulture, helping St. Louisans build community gardens and green spaces in their neighborhoods. There, Mimo met her friend and soon-to-be business partner, Miranda Duschack.

The business was officially established in 2012 when Mimo and Miranda purchased an historic flower farm dating to the 1870s. In this sale, they were able to obtain the land surrounding the condemned flower shop and original glass greenhouse, property comprising four contiguous lots. The farm has since expanded to occupy eight city lots spanning one acre. Further farm upgrades include restoring the original 1950s glass greenhouse and erecting high tunnels for more growing space, all which support their current day-to-day operations.

"Feed the soil and the soil will feed you."

A large part of Urban Buds's business model focuses on growing and marketing flowers year-round with farming methods aimed at extending the seasons with early spring bulbs, summer annuals and perennials, and late-season heirloom chrysanthemums.

Local flower shops and wedding event designers count on Urban Buds's high-quality anemones, delphinium, lisianthus, ranunculus, and dahlias, but the farm is also known for its own floristry.

OPPOSITE
Mimo's son August is growing up at Urban Buds. "This guy insists on coming to the farm and 'helping out,'" Mimo says. "He is a little kid with an old-school farmer's heart! My wish is that twenty years from now August will understand just how much he added to this family farm and know he helped build it."

Mimo and Miranda market and design with their flowers, promising couples their wedding bouquets, boutonnieres, and reception flowers are St. Louis-born and raised. "We try and educate clients so they know they are getting

Hard work produces beautiful blooms at Urban Buds. Mimo believes in immersing herself into the garden beds, to ensure that each bloom is picked at just the right time.

Dahlias harvested at the right time ensure a perfect bouquet.

"We are contributing to our community in a tangible way. People in the neighborhood walk by and tell us how beautiful things are here and we know our flowers encourage them to be aware and have a part in nature."

the best quality product for their very best day," Mimo says.

In addition to selling bouquets and bunches to farmers' market buyers, Urban Buds's "Petals On Our Porch" program supplies bulbs, plants, and cut flowers to customers who order from the online store for in-person pick-up at the farm. The popular "Best Buds" flower club is a six-week bouquet subscription program that routinely sells out. Participants also are invited to attend a members-only farm tour, an activity deepening their personal connection to locally grown flowers and the farmers who grow them.

"I call this the little engine that could, because we crank out a lot of flowers," Mimo says. "Urban farming is so fantastic for flowers because you can

really pack in a lot of blooms on a small property. We are contributing to our community in a tangible way. People in the neighborhood walk by and tell us how beautiful things are here and we know our flowers encourage them to be aware and have a part in nature, even in the city."

FAVORITE FLOWER. Mimo loves ranunculus, a gorgeous flower Urban Buds grows in the dead of winter when most nurseries are quiet and locally grown flowers are hard to come by. When temperatures are freezing outside, she finds it is a gift to walk into a 60-degree greenhouse and discover these beauties in full bloom in a spectrum of violet to white to magenta—an experience reinforcing how thrillingly beautiful she finds ranunculus.

Springtime inside the historic glass
house at Urban Buds. The restored
growing space extends the season for
early crops like ranunculus, delphinium,
and stock, which are popular with
local florists and designers.

BRON-ZURI HANSBORO

Floral Designer

RICHMOND, VIRGINIA

THE FLOWER GUY BRON

Bron-Zuri Hansboro, an award-winning floral designer and educator, is best known as the lead designer and owner of The Flower Guy Bron. An innovator and entrepreneur, his business takes a holistic and intuitive approach, providing bespoke design and styling experiences for weddings and events of all types. His studio has created a distinct brand of luxury based on the motto: "We don't sell flowers, we sell experiences."

BRON-ZURI HANSBORO did not predict a future for himself in flowers. Although his parents were in the military, the arts, including theater, were part of his upbringing. "I was not a child of privilege, but a child whose parents wanted me to be exposed to cultural activities."

As an early passion, Bron loved watching cooking and garden shows on television. He studied how menus and meals were presented, what to serve for different occasions, and various entertaining styles. As a teen using grocery store flowers, Bron experimented with floral design to accompany family meals. He befriended a few florists and wholesalers who sold him flowers, and eventually, Bron gained attention in his community for the floral arrangements he generously created for family and friends.

After earning a degree in sociology from Howard University in 2009, Bron accepted a position as an autism specialist for middle and high school students. This experience taught Bron how to understand his students'

verbal and nonverbal styles of communication. "I worked with one of the most fragile segments of society," he remembers. "I had to embody empathy and just be kind. Being gracious to all my students, as well as to other people along the way, no matter their situation, was and still is an important part of how I live and work today. The lessons and skills I acquired as a teacher have helped in my interactions with clients."

Bron was lured into his new profession like many flower enthusiasts whose talents are noticed and appreciated by others. In 2013, a friend asked Bron to create the florals for his wedding. He often had considered floral design as an additional income source and a respite from the demands of teaching. While he previously had created florals for small events and occasions, Bron viewed his first wedding commission as a monumental task.

That event served as a catalyst for more floral design requests, inspiring Bron to make the decision to resign as a teacher and form The Flower Guy

ABOVE
Creamy white and apricot bouquets for
a bride and attendants reflect Bron's
contemporary-chic styling and feature
roses, anthurium, eucalyptus, and ferns.

Bron in 2014. Floral design brought out his creativity, and his studio progressed far beyond that first wedding. He has produced hundreds of weddings in subsequent years, receiving multiple WeddingWire "Couple's Choice" awards, and being named to

"Stay in your own vase. Many in this industry want to be like others we see trending and we often forget our own authenticity. I am on a perpetual journey to remain authentic in an industry where people are constantly duplicating each other."

OPPOSITE
"When high fashion meets the ballroom," a signature centerpiece that elevates garden roses, spray roses, and hydrangea so they float gorgeously above the diners for a wedding reception.

Special Events magazine's "2019 Young Event Pros to Watch" list. He has been featured as an expert by *Brides* magazine and is a frequent speaker at the Wedding MBA Conference, recently presenting on "Affordable Floral Luxury" and tabletop designs. "My career did not start in fabulous ballrooms or with unlimited budgets. It started with a five-by-five-inch clear glass cube," he says with a grin. Today, however, those elegant ballrooms, destination estates, and romantic wineries are popular venues for The Flower Guy Bron's events.

In addition to wedding and event design, Bron is a mentor, dedicated to creating business opportunities for small and emerging vendors, from flower growers and florists to event planners. His full name, Bron-Zuri, means "the Source" in Swahili, a fitting reference to his industry leadership role as a source of support for his peers. Bron recognized the need for a safe online space for creatives in the floral and events industry, especially in 2020 and 2021 as many gatherings were postponed or cancelled. He created Ethos West Collective, an online community for Black wedding professionals in the United States and Europe. "I formed this group to provide a place for creatives to connect and find an accepting community," he says.

FAVORITE FLOWER. The peony is Bron's favorite flower. His grandmother Lilly grew the most beautiful peonies, which he remembers as a collection of more than thirty different perennial varieties. He recently transplanted most of these original herbaceous plants to his own garden for his future children to enjoy in the same way he did as a child. A soft pink ruffled peony is one of his favorites, along with a cultivar named Coral Charm.

Regal and elegant floral styling for a reception at the
historic John Marshall Ballrooms in Richmond, Virginia. Bron
explains, "The art of developing a lush tablescape centers
around building layers of colors, textures, and accessories."

DREW RIOS

Floral Designer

LOS ANGELES, CALIFORNIA

ROGUE & FOX FLORAL CO.

Drew Rios established Rogue & Fox Floral Co. to create unapologetically wild art, fulfilling her need to go rogue from the everyday. Her Los Angeles-based studio channels her desire to make modern floral art that embodies movement with boldness. Drew believes "color is always a good thing."

"UNDENIABLY AUTHENTIC" is how Drew Rios describes herself and her floral studio. She has worn many professional hats, from children's clothing designer and family services counselor, to accounting and financial planning professional, and even flower farmer. She also trained as a nurse, but found the work grueling. After letting her husband know she no longer found nursing fulfilling, he suggested she simply work with flowers. She recalled how much the experience of having flowers in her hands relieved stress and gave her life a sense of balance.

As an African American woman, Drew also recognized the challenge of entering floristry on her own terms, creating a business synonymous with her distinctive arrangements and event planning.

Drew grew up in Los Angeles in a loving family where both parents were present and supportive. She learned gardening from her father, who taught that her skills, not her race, should define her work. "I would follow him

ABOVE
A Mayesh Design Star for 2021, Drew created an enchanting, dark vibe for an avant-garde installation using fronds, ferns, moss, baby's breath, tropical foliage, and floral accents.

OPPOSITE
Baby's breath is a show-stopper for a styled shoot, with florals by Rogue & Fox Flower Co. Creative Director, The Co. Lab; Hair and Makeup, Salt Spell Beauty; Rental Studio, Table Method; Model, Austin Brown for NTA Model Management; and Location, Undefeated Creative.

TOP
Showing off her color confidence, Drew designed a whimsical tablescape to illustrate how to use grocery store flowers and fruits for unexpectedly gorgeous results.

BOTTOM
"This piece represents every reason why I decided to be a designer: Freedom. The freedom to create. The freedom to express my ideas. The freedom to go against the grain. The freedom to take risks. The freedom to just be. May we all shape the freedom we want."

eagerly, watching and asking questions about whatever he was doing," Drew remembers. "He would answer in short sentences and ask me questions, often allowing me to answer my original questions." Mastering many projects such as growing bonsai and designing koi ponds, her father's work in the garden planted seeds of wisdom he shared with all his children.

Drew couldn't help but notice a conspicuous lack of African Americans in the floral industry. The void motivated her to work harder developing Rogue & Fox Floral's reputation for dramatic designs unlike anything else in the market.

"There is room for everyone in the world of floriculture. Opportunities are opening up as people realize how much African American voices and creativity matter," Drew states. She also considers reaching out to smaller growers and minority florists in her community an important part of her work. Encouraging others to be true to their vision as florists has led to speaking engagements, teaching private workshops, and mentoring.

"I believe in elevating the voice of African Americans in floristry. It takes a community of people who come together to work together to accomplish a goal," she says. Ever evolving, one of Drew's current projects is called "Five Minutes with Flower Friends." In this project, Drew takes a few minutes to talk with floral growers, designers, or event planners, pursuing a deeper dive to broaden the conversation and expand possibilities for exposure. Rogue & Fox is more than just a florist; the business produces imaginative floral fantasies. The displays Drew and her team curate start out in her home studio. Ideas soon become real, leading to collaborations with fashion and lifestyle brands. She partnered with the athletic shoemaker Allbirds to create a botanical installation for the 2021 Los Angeles Marathon, and she frequently produces florals for videos and styled editorial photo shoots.

"Flowers came to me when I was buried in grief and despair. Creatively, I felt lost. Spiritually, I felt deprived. Flowers lifted me up and gave me the sense of purpose I longed for. They gave me life."

For more than ten years, Drew has focused on the art and creativity found in floral design—not the struggle. "Not everyone has a profound story of struggle," she says. "My family has been very supportive of my efforts and has been there to help me grow." Having a child with autism has given Drew another reason to make a difference for those facing challenges. She includes her son Dillon in floral preparation, deliveries, and other shop activities, preparing him to explore future paths and understand what hard work looks like. "I want him to know there is nothing that can't be accomplished, even if people hold you back due to their own fears. You can be fearless when you know your own worth."

FAVORITE FLOWER. Drew's favorite flower is the bearded iris, which encompasses power, boldness, and character. When designed en mass, its forms and hues evoke strength and depth. "Its beauty is fleeting, but always captivating," she says.

OPPOSITE
For a colorful and unconventional styled photo shoot, Drew explains her approach: "Paint with flowers but make it juicy."

JOY PROCTOR

Creative Director

PORTLAND, OREGON

JOY PROCTOR DESIGN

Joy Proctor is the owner and visionary behind Joy Proctor Design, a full-service studio specializing in destination weddings, commercial art direction, and special events. As a creative director, editorial and commercial stylist, and product designer, she believes in bringing fantasies to life. Joy has been named a top designer by Harper's *Bazaar*, *Vogue*, Martha Stewart, and *Brides*.

ABOVE
"A love story told in flowers. I can think of no better pairing than the pansy and the garden rose," Joy says of this bouquet featuring David Austin roses and pansies from her late spring garden.

OPPOSITE
Shortly before the Pantone colors of the year for 2016 were announced (Rose Quartz and Serenity), Joy designed this violet and blush bouquet. "The goal was to show a feminine color palette in a new and elegant way. The feature was published in *The Knot*, and little did we know it would be an example of the two colors of the year used together."

DEPENDING ON WHERE you want to begin the story of Joy Proctor—Eswatini (formerly Swaziland) in Southern Africa, or Canyonville, Oregon—this is a story about happiness, adventure, caring, and love. It makes sense a child named Joy could manifest a magical existence. Both places, Oregon and Eswatini, are held dear in Joy's heart because of family and location.

Joy attended the University of California, Santa Barbara and graduated with honors in political science. Thinking she would pursue law school, she worked as a paralegal, but soon realized this path wasn't for her. Joy resigned, found a part-time job, and advertised her services on Craigslist as a free wedding planner.

Floral design came almost intuitively when Joy's first client told her the table centerpieces were going to be "bowls of tortilla chips." She had a different artistic vision, purchasing vases from Goodwill, clipping flowers and branches from local gardens, and designing last-minute centerpieces. The change

OPPOSITE
Joy created this editorial design out of her love for the beauty and magic of Bali. The top is made of strung Jasmine flowers.

TOP
"Styling is more than an opportunity to create beauty, it is an opportunity to represent my background, dreams, and wishes visually." Hair and makeup designer Harold James.

BOTTOM
Joy styled this fashion shoot featuring a daffodil headpiece by Kiana Underwood of Tulipina; hair and makeup by Janet Villa; and gown by Zuhair Murad.

clearly pleased her client. "As a dreamer, I will go to the ends of the earth for something I believe in," Joy says. "I wanted to give the bride a positive memory of her table settings on such a special day." This was the beginning of Joy Proctor Designs, founded in 2007. "Beautiful flowers," she adds, "saved me from continuing to work in a job that was simply not for me."

Within four years of launching Joy Proctor Designs, she was one of Santa Barbara's most sought-after wedding planners, thanks in large part to having created and published styled photo shoots showcasing her aesthetic vision.

Today, Joy is known for producing original, inventive concepts and luxury destination weddings. With the aim of styling every commission as if for a magazine feature, Joy has designed and styled weddings and events in Italy, Provence, the Colorado resort town of Telluride, the Cotswolds, Thailand, and a number of destinations on the African continent, including South Africa, Zambia, Mozambique, and Eswatini. In 2017 and 2018, she

designed a capsule collection of luxury bridal footwear with Bella Belle shoes.

Joy's floral artistry is informed in part by the places of her youth, including the Pacific Northwest and Southern Africa. Her father left Oregon as a young man to join the Peace Corps, serving on assignments throughout Africa. He met Joy's mother, also an educator, in Eswatini, a place where little Joy could run free and play outside. When she was three, the family returned to the United States, and settled in Santa Barbara, by way of her grandparents' Oregon farm.

Success, talent, and confidence may seem to come to Joy naturally, but she personally has experienced racism in the wedding industry. "There are moments such as when a client who has not met me in person begins talking with my assistant as if I am not even there," she explains. "When I take charge of the situation, you can see their embarrassment for making an erroneous assumption that I'm not the boss. It took me a long time, as a Black woman who just happens to be

LEFT
Joy designed a Tuscan-inspired reception for her dear friend Kim Wiseley, editor of the wedding magazine *Flutter*. The color palette included warm watermelon, coral, and sunset tones paired against taupes and cremes as a nod to Kim and Tyler's engagement in Tuscany.

RIGHT
"In my workshops I talk a lot about how color and texture express emotion, and how as a designer I try to find ways to balance my use of color with neutrals. This lilac and blush cake by Maggie Austin is the perfect example, with feminine, joyful color balanced with subdued tones."

"Happiness is a choice. I chose event planning and floral design when I realized I did not want to work in an office. Flowers make me happy, so I chose what brings me joy."

biracial, to overcome self-doubt as I wondered whether my high-end clients really understood if I knew what I was doing for them. Now I know I am good enough and that not everybody has to be my client."

In 2020, Joy Proctor Designs worked with friends and florists in Portland to create the Say Their Names Memorial, leveraging Joy's event planning expertise to make an important impact. "My sister Elise Proctor and a team of her friends compiled the names of more than 200 African Americans whose lives were taken by systemic racism and racial injustice. We built two different portable exhibits so they could travel to displays around the country. I realized the conversations we were just beginning to have about race were long overdue and we need to have more of them. I wanted my business to help catapult change and action."

FAVORITE FLOWER. Pansies, especially lavender-colored ones. "The pansy is a happy plant that is so colorful, not to mention useful in many applications," she says. "I love how they are now being bred with longer stems for use in bouquets."

OPPOSITE
Joy was commissioned to design a wedding that blended the bride's Thai and Chinese heritage with the beauty and history of Budapest. "Culture, history, and setting never fail to inspire," she says.

DEE HALL

Flower Farmer

NORFOLK, VIRGINIA

MERMAID CITY FLOWERS

Dee Hall is the owner and creative mind behind the specialty cut-flower urban microfarm named Mermaid City Flowers. Her floral enterprise grows blooms for farmers' markets and for local customers. Dee follows sustainable, regenerative growing practices and has a special interest in native perennials.

"I want people to know my business is rooted in joy. I wanted to take something I love and share it. Flowers are beautiful but also serve such a practical environmental function. I feel lucky to be a steward of the garden."

Dahlias are one of Dee's signature flowers, shown blooming in
midsummer abundance in Mermaid City Flowers' cutting garden.

BORN IN BROOKLYN, Dee Hall eventually landed in Norfolk, Virginia, as an adult, bringing with her seeds of inspiration from an early childhood living in Saint Lucia, an island nation in the Caribbean, where lush green environments are a part of the natural landscape. Plant-filled memories of her childhood visits to spend time with her Saint Lucian relatives have inspired Dee's passion as a floral entrepreneur.

Prior to living in Norfolk, Dee pursued a career as a real estate property manager, moving around the country from New York to Texas to Virginia, but flowers were always on her mind. "I often found myself advising my clients on flowers and gardening," Dee says. While living in Virginia Beach for ten years, Dee continued to grow flowers, vegetables, and assorted herbs until an unexpected fire in 2018 transformed her life and precipitated her move to Norfolk the same year.

In Norfolk, she began to garden again, taking advantage of the near perfect growing climate in the Tidewater region of Virginia. At her new home, Dee planted fruit trees, berries, and flowers. While raising her favorite annual and perennial blooms, she began searching for locally grown flowers for her upcoming wedding ceremony. "I was shocked to find virtually no resource for locally grown flowers," Dee recalls. A competent gardener, she immediately saw a void waiting to be filled.

Acting on her inspiration, Dee established Mermaid City Flowers as an urban cut-flower garden, adding her locally grown blossoms to Norfolk's thriving scene of artists, growers, and makers. "I named my business after the great waterside city of Norfolk, which has the nickname of Mermaid City," she says. "There are mermaid sculptures all over town and I feel like the name gives a glint of magic and polish to all things here."

Mermaid City Flowers grows and markets specialty cut flowers through a floral subscription service and creates everyday floral arrangements for local patrons. Dee also encourages collaboration in her community through The

"There is no easier way for me to engage with the world around me than to step out into the garden. Flowers have always surrounded me; I do not remember a life without them, and I never want to have it any other way."

Tidewater Flower Collective, an organization providing continuing farming education, farm visits, and efforts to connect consumers with the source of their flowers. With more than twenty members, the collective also supports cost-sharing for supplies and jointly provides flowers for large events.

Ever mindful of the challenges of being a woman of color in the world of floristry, Dee has created an online virtual community of Black specialty cut-flower farmers, found on Instagram as @blackflowerfarmers. "We have found strength in numbers and through knowledge-sharing with those whose hands have been in the soil for longer than I have, including participants with so many different areas of expertise. To me, this is magical!"

As a board member of the Norfolk Botanical Garden, Dee focuses on advancing the cause of inclusivity and diversity. The hands of more than 200 African American women cleared the land and planted flowers and shrubs, making this garden significant to Virginia history. As she so eloquently observes, "What has captured my soul about gardening is its ability to connect people at anytime, anywhere."

FAVORITE FLOWER. Dahlias are special to Dee because they were the initial catalyst for her business. Anthuriums are also one of her favorites, a species grown by Dee's grandmother and a signature flower in her arrangements. Seeing them reminds Dee of the shared legacy of sweat from many brows.

NICOLE CORDIER

Botanical Artist	HAWAII
	CORDIER BOTANICAL ART, GRACE FLOWERS HAWAII

Nicole Cordier is a botanical artist who explores the power of nature and the earth's elemental forces of light and fire, often combined with cultivated and wild-gathered flowers. She is known for her temporal floral installations, created and then captured on film. Nicole is also a manager at Grace Flowers Hawaii, an environmentally conscious, full-service florist in Honoka'a, Hawaii.

For her "Life. Death. Rebirth." series, Nicole's depiction of "death" is symbolized by "a column of beheaded thorny rose stems wrapped in equally thorny blackberry vines sitting on a bed of varying shades of red rose petals and burning red candles, which I thought, properly conveyed my feelings towards heartbreak."

BY MERGING HER scientific training with an impulse to create, Nicole Cordier makes botanical art in response to her own curiosity about the natural world. Nicole's most notable installation pieces have been entirely self-funded and produced during in-between hours while free-lancing as a floral designer. In 2012, while living in Seattle and serving as one of the first staff members at the Seattle Wholesale Growers Market Cooperative, Nicole produced "Life. Death. Rebirth." an evocative, three-dimensional installation in equal parts both sculptural and botanical, capturing the temporal qualities of the heart through petals, leaves, moss, and branches. "I wanted the viewer to experience the stages of love through a floral palette," she explains.

In 2013, Nicole produced "Prism Project" and photographed the composition in a darkened room, using entirely white Pacific Northwest flow-ers. She arranged a beam of light to shine through a prism, casting a living ribbon of colors onto the flowers, distorting the lines between literal and imaginative. Nicole describes her aesthetic as "wild, yet orderly," saying, "My work can be systematic, but always with an element of the wild." Because she infuses the theme of light into her work, Nicole is intensely aware of how light changes the way we see color and texture.

Nicole's botanical art is now influenced by the flora of Hawaii, where she has lived with her husband and son since 2014. She works closely with Alison Grace Higgins, owner of Grace Flowers Hawaii, where Nicole is a manager. The shop's services are in high demand, as the fifteen-person team provides everyday flowers and plants to residents of the Big Island and floral design services for destination weddings.

They set aside time to stretch their creativity with editorial-styled photo sessions, including a Polynesian-inspired botanical couture collection for American Flowers Week in 2018, and, more recently, a floral flashback

to 1960s Hawaii, where Nicole and others served as models.

Flowers weren't an obvious career path for someone majoring in geology at the University of Colorado, Boulder. In 2001, as a sophomore needing a part-time job, Nicole became a delivery driver for a small florist. Mesmerized by the botanicals she delivered, including the tiniest details of specific blooms, she began imagining ways they might be artfully arranged.

After college, Nicole briefly considered opening a flower shop, but without start-up capital, she didn't know how to pursue the idea. Instead, she joined a geological software firm, which gave her financial security and the resources to travel to places like New Zealand and Vietnam. The pull of a lost creative life lingered, though. "Ultimately, my idea of engaging with the earth did not involve sitting behind a computer. As a woman of color, I always felt slightly uncomfortable in the world of geology. While I enjoyed the benefits as well as the pay, I also wanted to have a feeling

The original arrangement for Nicole's "Burning Bouquet" project,
featuring a dramatic banksia flower with its zigzag foliage, hydrangeas,
citrus foliage, and hapu'u fern in a coconut flower embrace.

For her "Burning Bouquet" project, Nicole created a mock-up; several
months later, after the flowers had dried, she burned the piece and
asked a photographer to capture the fleeting moment on film.

"The world of floristry offers a special place where diversity makes a difference in every arrangement. There is always something new and exciting to work with."

of belonging to a community of like-minded people."

In 2009, a friend she met while traveling invited Nicole to move to Seattle. The move reunited her with flowers and she eventually landed a job at the Seattle Wholesale Growers Market Cooperative, which at the time, was an emerging farmer-owned hub for Pacific Northwest cut flowers. "Working there was really the building block to my new creative life," she recalls. "It was mind-blowing. I learned so much and the people I met—flower farmers and other designers—exposed me to many different ways to work with flowers. It was a pivotal point for me."

Living and working in Hawaii has allowed Nicole to further broaden her botanical palette as she explores the relationship between science and art through flowers. "I used to think Hawaii would offer only tropical blossoms. My thoughts have now changed as I continue to embrace the floral biodiversity here—and I'm stimulated creatively," she says. "In floral design, I have found a universal acceptance where I can unquestionably be myself and view myself as an artist."

FAVORITE FLOWER. Nicole loves the lotus, an ancient plant that has endured centuries. "It's so incredibly perfect-looking to me," she says. "I find the way the lotus unassumingly evolves from a less than perfect environment, rising gracefully on slender stems, and then opening into perfect blooms, simply amazing."

ABOVE

The "Prism Project" blends Nicole's fascination
with light, geology, and botanicals. She shone light
from a prism onto the surface of an all-white floral
installation, with polychromatic results. "It's amazing
what you see when you look closely," she says.

HANNAH MORGAN

Floral Designer

SEATTLE, WASHINGTON

FORTUNATE ORCHARD

Hannah Morgan is owner and lead designer of Fortunate Orchard, a seasonal floral design studio founded in 2016 to reflect the botanical character of the Pacific Northwest. Hannah incorporates locally sourced materials, some direct from her own garden, as well as material grown in the United States, to create arrangements designed to bring outdoor beauty inside.

HANNAH MORGAN LIKES TO SAY she has "a bachelor of fine arts degree in one hand and a pair of pruning shears in the other." Her designs are deeply rooted in the seasons of the Pacific Northwest and much of her botanical arrangements, wreaths, garlands, and commercial installation work comes from the Fortunate Orchard garden, steps away from her worktable. Hannah and her family live on Orchard Terrace, a tiny street in South Seattle.

"When we moved here, the previous owners had hung a sign on the garage reading 'Fortunate Orchard.' I'm not sure what it referred to, but we've used it as our estate's name, with a wink, because our estate is a 900-square-foot house on a city lot. Since I use my garden so much for inspiration and floral products, I wanted the name to be rooted in this place, because my business couldn't exist without the garden I've worked to create for so many years."

The path leading Hannah from art school, where she focused on

119

printmaking, to floral design is apparent today, but it was not a direct one. "I was doing a lot of printmaking, which was also my first foray into business ownership. I had a card company for a couple years until motherhood became a priority.

"There is a similar approach between the printmaking work I did and the floral work I do now. Printmaking is very egalitarian—it's available to

everyone. I wanted my art to be accessible and in people's hands. And I've found the parallel with floral design because I'm exploring how to bring flowers and plants into people's lives on a daily basis."

Hannah jokes that like many art school graduates, she landed in the restaurant industry. A friend knew about Hannah's phenomenal garden at her home and asked if she could create something

OPPOSITE
At the peak of summer, dahlias take center stage in the Fortunate Orchard cutting garden, with support from a row of summer annuals. "Every single time I pick up a pair of clippers and begin a design, I marvel how I get to do this for other people."

TOP
A refreshing spring bouquet designed with peonies, ranunculus, bridal wreath viburnum, sweet peas, and double columbine blooms.

BOTTOM
Some of Hannah's best design ingredients are close at hand, clipped from her Seattle garden, like these delicate clematis tendrils.

Colorful blooms creatively wrap the base and hug the rough-
hewn beams that form the arch for this woodland wedding.

"Find beauty in the unexpected."

for her restaurant's entryway. "As I arranged florals, I never before realized how my art degree would play a role in how I interpret the beauty found in nature," she reflects.

This unexpected opportunity became a way for Hannah to use her degree, continue to care for her two children, and provide income to her household. Her garden is both canvas and palette as she develops her modern, naturalistic aesthetic.

Fortunate Orchard has expanded from providing floral installations for restaurant clients to designing for weddings and events and building a following for custom-made arrangements, which Hannah personally delivers. "I noticed the emotional impact flowers can have on people. It also helped me realize what I want to do more of, as well as less of. I feel like I am doing what allows me to be true to myself."

Entering the floral industry as a second career has given Hannah more confidence in selecting projects reflecting who she is. "My work is a form of

art and it can't be twisted to fit into something that doesn't speak to me. This mindset enables me to work with clients who seek out and value my aesthetic, rather than viewing me only as a florist providing for their event."

Hannah's floral style is dramatic, unruly, yet colorfully creative, making it distinct to her personality. Hannah's family—with its Filipino, African American, and white relatives—is as diverse as the plants in her abundant garden. "With the current awareness of racial inequities still existing, this new attention has elevated the success of minority businesses," she notes. "It has been helpful finding other Black people in this industry, artists who I might not ever have known. Visual representation is so very important as a connector."

FAVORITE FLOWER. Every flower has a place, depending on the season. "A new lisianthus cultivar has captured my heart right now. It has a small purple bloom, mauve with a deep-colored center. Every time I use it in arrangements, the result is simply elegant."

NATASHA GRAHAM

Flower Farmer

MARIPOSA, CALIFORNIA

YOSEMITE FLOWER FARM

Natasha Graham started Yosemite Flower Farm in 2020. The small-scale flower farm uses no-till, organic practices to grow a wide selection of cut flowers Natasha sells weekly at nearby farmers' markets. Yosemite Flower Farm also maintains a Community Supported Agriculture (CSA) floral subscription program and offers local flower deliveries.

Yosemite Flower Farm's tidy row of
zinnias will soon be incorporated into
bouquets and bunches for local fans.

BY THE TIME she embraced flower
farming, Natasha Graham had spent
more than two decades living in San
Francisco, working in both the culinary world and in technology sales.
Professional success enabled Natasha
and her husband to purchase a home
in the foothills of the Sierra Nevada
Mountains, about 170 miles east of San
Francisco in the remote community
of Mariposa, 40 miles from Yosemite
National Park. The property is reached
by following an unpaved, two-mile
road leading to a five-acre vineyard surrounding a berm-style house built into
the mountain, its design ensuring cool
interiors during average summer temperatures of 80-90 degrees Fahrenheit.

The couple originally acquired the
property in 2018, and although Natasha
enjoyed weekend visits while they
completed renovation work, she had
no plans to permanently relocate.

"This was just supposed to be an
investment property. My husband
came out here for four months to work
on the house and then he didn't want

to come back to San Francisco," she laughs. "I'm completely a city girl—I was raised in Los Angeles—and I told him, 'I'm not moving there!'"

Natasha had tended a garden of food and flowers in her San Francisco backyard, and she described herself as a "farmers' market groupie" during the years she worked in the Bay Area, waiting tables, cooking, and managing various restaurants. Her favorite culinary job was as nutritional chef for the YMCA. "I'd go to food banks and do live demonstrations to show people how to use the vegetables, fruit, and other produce in their meals, and then write up my recipes to share. Besides farming, it was probably the best job I've ever had because I was teaching people."

The road to flower farming followed the loss of her mother in 2016, which, understandably, left Natasha seeking a change of pace as well as time to heal. "I noticed every time I would drive away from San Francisco and head here to the Sierra foothills I felt no stress

or anxiety until I returned to the city. A lot of that stress came from living in San Francisco's big city intensity." After commuting back and forth for an entire year, Natasha's attitude changed and, in December 2019, she decided to call Mariposa her full-time home.

Bolstered by her husband's encouragement, Natasha realized her depression over the loss of her mother dissolved when she spent time in the garden. "I was getting up really early to start my day at four or five in the morning. And I was out there until way past dark," she recalls. "It made me so happy just to see the growth of my plants and the seasons change in the garden."

The idea of transforming the Mariposa garden into a flower farm originally seemed like a way to market their property as a pretty vacation rental. "The rental idea still hasn't happened," Natasha explains. "But things kind of steamrolled as I discovered how therapeutic gardening was." In January 2020, she enrolled in an online flower farming class and soon established

"Flowers gave me a reason to get up in the morning and live."

Yosemite Flower Farm to grow zinnias, cosmos, sunflowers, roses, dahlias, and other vibrant, heat-loving flowers. Natasha had early success selling her blooms at farmers' markets, but admittedly, she felt isolated from other flower farmers.

Through Instagram, she discovered Aishah Lurry, and a floral sisterhood blossomed. "Daily contact with Aishah was like having a great friend by my side in the garden as I built my business," Natasha says. "She helped me strategize ideas for creative marketing, for locating places to sell, and was a comforting voice as I navigated this new journey. I had the ambition and the drive, but I needed to connect with someone who was pursuing a similar path."

Natasha knows there have been many historical and systemic obstacles for African Americans to enjoy the fullness and beauty of nature in this country.

"To be an African American flower farmer, to grow and sell what brings joy to others, is quite meaningful to me. I want to show what success looks like so more African Americans can connect with nature, own land, and establish farms."

FAVORITE FLOWER. Natasha's favorite flower is the ranunculus. "This beautiful flower has single and double blooms in unexpected color combinations," she says. "While some think it has a delicate appearance, it's quite tough and makes a wonderful addition to any bouquet."

OPPOSITE
Natasha's flower harvest is an explosion of color, texture, and form and includes dahlias, gomphrena, and lisianthus.

ISHA FOSS

Floral Designer

VIRGINIA BEACH, VIRGINIA

ISHA FOSS DESIGN

Isha Foss and her team at Isha Foss Design provide full-service event design, including the flowers. A love of fine furnishings and tasteful interiors influences Isha's approach to stylish floral and events, reflecting their clients' personalities and stories in settings just right for them.

ISHA FOSS FELL INTO floral and event design after leaving a successful career in information technology. Like many professional women with children, a forced pause in the form of an employer buyout eventually caused Isha to explore a different, and more artistic, profession.

The roots of Isha Foss Design began twenty years ago when Isha, newly departed from the corporate world, volunteered at a women's shelter near her home in Virginia Beach, Virginia. She gained experience managing fundraising events for the nonprofit organization, readily transferring her IT project management skills to her own planning business, while also raising her son Miles and newborn daughter Hope. "I was supposed to be a stay-at-home mom doing the occasional wedding coordination, and I booked three clients my first year. This led to fifteen clients the following year and something like forty events the third year. I've designed for forty to fifty weddings every year since," she explains.

Out of necessity, floral design became a signature service of Isha Foss Design. "I found myself planning an event, selecting linens and other items, and then the flowers we'd ordered wouldn't be what I had in mind," she says. "It was never what I imagined in my head, so I started designing flowers to complete the event."

When she plans a fancy party or elegant wedding, Isha often thinks back to her Detroit childhood. As a girl, she was fascinated with the opulent mansions originally built by automobile magnates in an area of Detroit known as Indian Village. As an adult, she conjured her own interpretation of the parties and decor that might have taken place within the walls of those elegant homes.

Extravagant events became her trademark. "My aesthetic is 'updated traditional,'" Isha explains. "That's where the memories of mansions come in. In Detroit, these old houses had a different life from a different time. I love the fabric wallpaper, crystal doorknobs, and crystal chandeliers found within

LEFT
Singular sensation: an updated classic cascading
bridal bouquet featuring white phalaenopsis orchids.

RIGHT
Isha gathered white peonies, sweet peas,
parrot tulips, and ranunculus with sprigs of
lepidium for a dreamy spring bridal bouquet.

ABOVE
Isha Foss designed the lovely blue and
white florals for custom screening
panels fabricated by Blue Steel Lighting
Design for a wedding at Norfolk's
Hermitage Museum and Gardens.

many of these buildings. I am not a minimalist! Give me linens, flowers, a hundred different candles, and hotel silver. You can be eating fried chicken on that plate, but I just want a pretty plate, with a gold rim, please."

"I kept evolving in my service offerings until I stumbled upon the thing that felt like joy. Everything I do in my business is aimed at moving me to the point where I can stand at my design table and create."

Isha has studied with leading designers in the profession, plus she is a long-time member of the Chapel Designers, a collective of wedding and event designers. She recently expanded her award-winning studio, adding interior design, plant-scaping, and local flower deliveries under the Lynnhaven Florist brand (a reference to the name of her Virginia Beach neighborhood) to its diverse lineup of services.

Isha's clients and designs have appeared in magazines and blogs, including *The Knot*, *VOWS*, *Bridal Guide*, *Essence*, Style Me Pretty, *Ruffled*, and *Martha Stewart Weddings*, and she has designed flowers for the White House in Washington, DC.

Noticing the lack of people of color in the floristry industry, Isha says she has become even more determined to create distinctive and memorable designs for every event. "I am very aware I need to encourage other budding florists to step forward and share their talents."

With this intent, Isha is dedicating time to work with interns of color and expose them to career possibilities in floral design, including offering a paid mentoring program to encourage more diverse faces in the profession.

"I want people to not be surprised to see me when I represent Isha Foss Design. It is not only about the flowers, but also about the experience. I'm going to bring the pretty part. You just provide the emotion part and I'll create the background and the frame for your event, so you can fully be you in your moment."

FAVORITE FLOWER. Isha absolutely loves the delicate fanciness of a white scabiosa, also known as white pincushion flower. "Its daisy-like blossoms are so sweet, serving as a queen holding court over my arrangements."

WHITNEY JAYE

Flower Farmer

LITHONIA, GEORGIA

SUNBIRD FLOWERS

Sunbird Flowers is a family-owned flower farm nestled in Lithonia, Georgia. Run by Whitney Jaye and Brandon Stephens, the farm's mission is clear and deeply rooted in their family's agricultural legacy and spiritual work: to serve as stewards of the land and to bring joy and healing to communities through the splendor of locally, beautifully curated flowers.

WHITNEY JAYE DEFINES HERSELF as a "returning generation farmer," a term reflecting the renaissance of primarily younger Black farmers who are reclaiming the legacy of agriculture on their own terms.

Devoted to farming since 2012, Whitney Jaye and her partner Brandon Stephens started Sunbird Flowers in 2017, while also pursuing vegetable production at Semente Farm. In 2020, she received a scholarship to attend the Floret Flowers Online Workshop, which led them to shift their business to exclusively produce flowers.

"I think those of us who grow cut flowers are a particular type of farmer because most farmers either grow row-crop commodities or vegetables," Whitney Jaye points out. "Black farmers are already a small population and Black flower farmers are an even smaller segment of our community. I feel a kinship with others who choose flowers, because I recognize it's not an easy option for everybody, especially when growing food products and being able to provide food resources for

Black communities is so valuable. It's not an easy choice to say, 'I'm actually going to grow something people don't see as a necessity,' despite the fact it very much is.'"

The response to their flowers has affirmed their decision to plant dahlias, zinnias, celosias, gomphrena, amaranth, and other crowd-pleasing blooms. Whitney Jaye and Brandon's first season in full-time flower production included a waitlisted flower CSA partnership with a local restaurant in Atlanta. Since then, Sunbird Flowers has partnered with a beauty company to provide flowers and herbs as ingredients for the company's product line.

"When we switched to flowers, people were like, 'Yes!', which means for us, defining our success came in two ways: experiencing the positive response from customers as we changed our direction toward flowers, and then completing our entire first season as a full-time flower farm."

Growing flowers has a cultural significance going far beyond simply fulfilling market demand. To Whitney Jaye, flowers and herbs are a necessity, especially when used in medicines and for funerals, ceremonies, and other rituals. When Whitney Jaye and Brandon began growing flowers, it was meaningful for family members and people from their community to request their flowers at their key life moments, including home-goings of those who had died.

"Every time we went to a home-going, people talked about the food at the repast, people talked about the program, but almost nobody talked about the fact that across space, time, and geography, each person believed it was important to have flowers at each of these funerals. I would like to help connect those dots when we talk about what it means for Black people to self-determine around all aspects of our culture."

Every day on the farm looks different for this couple, who are raising their toddler son on eight acres shared with Brandon's family. From caring for their son and growing and harvesting flowers, to working full-time as the Director of Strategic and Programmatic

"Being a Black flower farmer means being a 'possibility model.' It also means knowing I bring forth joy and pleasure in the world. We get to be a part of these important life events. We are agents of happiness and beauty; this is an important contribution. It's never frivolous."

Development for the Southeastern African American Farmers Organic Network (SAAFON), Whitney Jaye is motivated by a responsibility to serve as steward for the land and the ecosystem they farm.

Well aware of the small number of contemporary Black flower farmers, she values elders such as Mimo Davis of Urban Buds for providing a valuable role model, along with mentors such as Jamila Norman of Patchwork City Farm. "Seeing examples of intentional, productive, exceptionally skilled flower growers helps me realize this can be viable work. I think the perception of [flower farming] as just frolicking through a field of flowers is so absurd, and Mimo really solidified in my mind this is a niche, one requiring skill. For

me, this also means knowing what I represent for other people. It reminds me when we return to a relationship with the land in an intuitive way, we can reimagine our connection—we can feel whole and healed."

FAVORITE FLOWER. It's all about Tecolote ranunculus, which to Whitney Jaye looks like a poppy mixed with ranunculus.

Interview and profile contributed by Myriah Towner.

OPPOSITE
Sunbird Flowers has come full circle for Whitney Jaye and her partner Brandon Stephens, as they now grow specialty cut flowers on land Brandon's family has tended for years.

KIARA HANCOCK

Floral Designer

SEATTLE, WASHINGTON

K. HANCOCK DESIGN

Kiara Hancock is the owner of K. Hancock Design, founded in 2014. She believes modern and romantic designs can coexist in harmony, and she brings weddings to life by making them resonate with joy. "The act of delivering positive memories of a joyful occasion or moment is worth its weight in gold," she says.

ABOVE
"Breakout," Kiara's audition piece fo HBO's *Full Bloom*, season two. She recreated the two-sided piece for the first episode of the season.

KIARA HANCOCK ESTABLISHED K. Hancock Design as a full-service wedding planning, design, and coordination studio. Naturally charismatic, she was a breakout personality on the second season of *Full Bloom* on HBO Max, which aired in 2021. "The floral design reality competition felt both exhilarating and stressful," Kiara recalls. "It was fun, but also quite a surreal experience. One of the most important lessons I learned was about myself. My love of floral arranging is not rooted in competition." This belief was expressed in the show's first episode, when contestants were asked to create a signature floral design to express their personal aesthetic, a challenge Kiara won.

She titled her piece "Breakout." "I wanted to design something representing where I come from. I'm from Milwaukie, Wisconsin, which is a really segregated place. It was one of the first places to declare racism as a public health crisis. The cinder blocks I used were like a 'gritty concrete jungle' and they explode with brilliant blue flowers, representing the joy I now welcome and chase in my life."

As a child, Kiara wasn't interested in her mother's vegetable garden or the nearby community garden plot, a fact she now finds ironic, considering how her husband Phil Hancock has a degree in agronomy and crop science and is a superintendent at a local golf course. They have developed a family garden of their own and even contemplated planting and growing cut flowers for Kiara's events.

When she was growing up, tennis and dancing were Kiara's favorite activities. After high school, she landed and won

TOP LEFT
Stunning and sultry, an installation features fluffy blooms of *Cotinus coggygria*, also called the purple smoketree.

BOTTOM RIGHT
Details like custom table number signs are part of K. Hancock Designs' full-service planning.

TOP RIGHT/BOTTOM LEFT
With an eye for creating beauty, harmony, and love in all of her designs, the colors chosen for this event draw attendees to gather and sit for awhile.

"When you feel as though there is no place for you at the table, build your own table. Make your own way in life as I have."

an audition to join the Seattle Seahawks' cheerleading team, with which she performed for nearly a decade. In addition to dance, working as an executive assistant allowed Kiara to learn logistics, event planning, and other skills essential for running a successful business.

One year after forming K. Hancock Events, Kiara won a scholarship to attend "Elements of Event Design," a workshop taught by Steve Moore of Seattle-based Sinclair & Moore, a

SEVEN

PREVIOUS
Kiara produced this dinner party installation for Modern
Love Seattle in 2019, a collaborative wedding event
that invites creatives to design for the contemporary
couple. Natural elements, a palette of muted and bright
pastels, and coordinated tabletop accessories hint
at a luxury destination like Marrakesh or Mexico.

celebrated luxury and destination wedding designer. "That's really the first time I touched flowers," she recalls. "Steve has been a great support to me and a great advocate of my business as I learn to say 'yes' to things and then figure them out."

Having a mentor like Steve Moore has also helped Kiara grow into her personal style and identify how her brand appears. "It was difficult finding other African American florists to connect with, and when I did, it was often on social media. As most African Americans know, we are often underrepresented in many professional situations. It was important to see someone who looked like me in this profession, and yet, I also have had a sense of being the most unique person in the room."

Kiara loves connecting with floral and events customers who appreciate her aesthetic style. "It's always exciting when someone lets me run wild and play with forms and colors," she admits, recognizing how her dance training continues as an ongoing influence. "I

like my floral elements to feel alive. When stems are jutting out, with a lot of movement, when they relate to each other in the composition—it's just like the gestures of dancers."

Kiara has been featured in *Vogue* and was named one of The Knot's "Ones to Watch." "We are going through a cultural revolution at this very moment," she shares. "It is a change I embrace, and it is long overdue. As an African American in this industry, I know there are some of us who are still afraid to show who we are. It is time to share who we are and find our audience."

FAVORITE FLOWER. Tulips are without a doubt Kiara's favorite flower. "Tulips are like caterpillars in the flower world. One day they are standing tall, the next morning they are elegantly draping in place. They are transformational, yet still provide a sort of evolving beauty."

TAIJ & VICTORIA COTTEN

| Flower Farmers | PITTSBORO, NORTH CAROLINA |
| | COTTENPICKED, LLC |

Taij and Victoria Cotten gained hands-on experience by working with local farms and participating in several local markets. This knowledge is what inspired them to start their own farm with cut flowers and more. The Cotten's are quite popular throughout the community for their bouquets, special occasion arrangements, florals for weddings, as well as a wholesale floral resource. They now own CottenPicked, LLC, a flower farm that is intentionally creating a legacy for their children.

TAIJ AND VICTORIA COTTEN are modern-day farmers who have created an agricultural lifestyle vastly different from their own childhoods. At their former jobs, they grew flowers and vegetables and raised pasteurized chickens, while also parenting their daughter Carleigh and son Titus. It was on this thirty-year-old organic farming entity that the Cottens gained invaluable skills and knowledge. The experience of farming for someone else was the fertilizer required for them to step out on faith and begin a new journey of their own.

"Most people do not 'get' our story," Victoria says. "We don't see other Black farmers actively farming for profit. We don't even see other African American farmers who have generationally continued to farm," she continues.

"We consider ourselves simply farmers," she says. "We are a family farming in an area rich in resources, in a community that embraces us for who we are."

Taij and Victoria are writing a new agricultural chapter about who gets to be a farmer. "We now live on Victoria's

family land. Our prior experience learning from experienced farmers has been excellent for us," Taij says. "Victoria's family is allowing us to establish a farm here. We are now officially CottenPicked, LLC."

After growing up in the small town of Pittsboro (located about forty miles west of Raleigh), dating, and

"Things come full circle. The first farm we ever visited provided us with the experience of a lifetime. Now we are investing in our own future on family land. This is such a feeling of freedom and allows us to be authentically who we are—Black flower farmers. We are not farming because it's the 'new' trend. We chose farming, specifically farming flowers."

LEFT
A field in peak bloom. The Cottens have fully embraced their dream of owning land and creating their own farm. With their children at their side, their dream is quickly becoming a reality.

welcoming their first child, the Cottens were determined to define their life purpose together.

"Neither of us knew exactly what we wanted to do," Taij explains. "Victoria just wanted to do something well and be great at it. She had attended North Carolina State University and was fascinated with food and bringing people together. I attended barber school and wanted to follow a path of entrepreneurship, but we both had found ourselves working in the restaurant industry." By the time of their daughter's birth in 2014, they knew that the race to the "top" would look different for them.

In 2016, the couple planned their own wedding ceremony, looking at venues and thinking about menus and flowers. "All the wedding venues we visited were farms," Victoria says. "That's when it all started coming together for Taij and me. We noticed that we worked together really well, and we liked being creative. In our perfect world we saw ourselves living on a farm where others could come, have events, and eat 'our' food and enjoy 'our' flowers."

Their informal research led to Craigslist jobs at a local flower shop during Mother's Day, picking up farmhand work, and taking classes in sustainable agriculture at Central Carolina Community College. "We discovered we were living in a farming mecca," Victoria says. "It became our mission to visit every farm here and talk with any farmer who possibly needed help and learn whatever they could offer. We knew then that a farm was in our future, to create legacy and wealth for our children."

RIGHT
The one-on-one time Taij and Titus have is important. Moments like this enforce a love of the land and the passion for farming as a profession.

Fast forward to 2021, and Taij and Victoria marvel at how much their lives have changed. The Cottens are in the process of moving to Victoria's family land to make their dream come true. Farming full-time for work, starting a farm from scratch, and being a young, active family certainly has its challenges. "Capital is the biggest challenge," says Victoria. In the fall of 2023, the Cottens started Cottenpicked, LLC, as the seed, while preparing for the bigger dream. "Farming is our freedom and is empowering. I carried our son for thirty-nine weeks while farming and, although hard work, I realized flower farming is something I enjoy. Having the opportunity to farm on family land allows us to be the family we want to be. Owning our own farm is the perfect opportunity to sow into the future for our children."

"We are intentionally generating a farming operation that will provide a certain level of wealth for our children. They will be able to say their parents did something different—and it worked,"

Taij says. "We wake up every day just to 'farm' and create other agricultural products, such as wreaths and seasonal decor. Our hard work is recognized by our peers—even though we're just kids from the small town of Pittsboro. This was never the dream, and now we couldn't imagine a world without it."

FAVORITE FLOWER. Taij loves celosia, with its spikes and the many vibrant varieties. Victoria loves all the flowers she grows, especially varieties with strong fragrances, including tuberose and stock. She is also enthralled by lisianthus. "We grow lizzies outdoors. No hoops. No protection. Growing lisianthus teaches patience," she says.

KAIFA ANDERSON-HALL

Horticultural Therapist

WASHINGTON, DC

PLANTS AND BLOOMS REIMAGINED

Kaifa Anderson-Hall is a horticultural therapist. She is also founder and CEO of the nonprofit organization Plants and Blooms ReImagined (PBR). PBR provides a therapeutic horticultural experience using donated and repurposed indoor plants and flowers, and enhances the well-being of diverse and underserved communities.

A sought-after speaker on the health and wellness benefits of plants and flowers, Kaifa is a leader in horticultural therapy circles as she establishes and facilitates horticultural therapy programs for diverse populations throughout the DC region.

KAIFA ANDERSON-HALL connects others to nature through horticultural therapy. Her organization, Plants and Blooms ReImagined, combines her social work training and her expertise working with public gardens, community gardens, and youth gardening programs. Plants and Blooms ReImagined is on a mission to reclaim, repurpose, and reimagine how flowers and plants can enhance the quality of everyday life, especially the lives of the most vulnerable.

Kaifa graduated from the University of Maryland, Baltimore with a degree in social work, and for many years she incorporated lessons from the garden and from growing herbs and flowers into her clinical services. In 2005, after finishing training as a District of Columbia Master Gardener, she returned to the Washington Youth Garden, first as a volunteer, and later joining full-time as program director.

"It was like going home again, being able to give back to a program that had given so much to me," she recalls.

In 2014, Kaifa obtained her Horticulture Therapy (HT) certification from the Horticultural Therapy Institute in Denver, which has allowed her to "reimagine" how she's serving her community. HT is the evidence-based practice of facilitating nature-based experiences to enhance overall wellness. Kaifa has sought ways to foster accessible plant- and flower-centered experiences, particularly for marginalized and vulnerable communities.

One catalyst for Plants and Blooms ReImagined came about during a community garden meeting at a friend's house. Buckets of flowers filled the living room, and when asked about their origin, the host shared how a floral designer friend had retrieved them after a client's wedding. "The host was hoping we'd help her find homes for them," Kaifa remembers. "All throughout the meeting I was simply marveling at the buckets of beautiful blooms, imagining how this could be a valuable, sustainable, and environmentally conscious source of flowers."

She has since put her idea into action and continues to forge relationships with designers, florists, and growers, allowing them to engage in more environmentally and socially conscious end-of-use practices by donating flowers from weddings and corporate functions, as well as surplus from their fields. The flowers are lovingly "reimagined" twofold—recreated as small bouquets delivered to assisted living facilities and other nonprofit organizations across Washington, DC, or prepped and used for PBR's therapeutic floral HT program.

Rather than a physician writing a prescription for a pharmaceutical to "solve" a health problem, Kaifa writes an altogether more wholistic prescription through plants: "I call it a 'prescription in a bloom'!" In 2018, the American Horticultural Society honored Kaifa with a Great American Gardener Award for her contributions to the field of horticultural therapy. Additionally, Kaifa and her work were most recently recognized when she was named one of nine recipients

"From a very young age flowers called out to me from the storefronts. I did not know all about what was going on inside, because I did not have the opportunity to experience a flower shop until my senior year in high school. But somehow, I knew, something magical was happening on the other side of the doors! Call it flower magic!"

of the District of Columbia's 2021 Sustainability Awards.

Kaifa's concept of a "Bloom Mobile" (inspired by seeing a Blood Mobile and subconsciously transposing the "d" in "Blood" for an "m" in "Bloom"), is her ultimate goal, a mission that will allow her to further engage with under-served communities where they are by bringing the benefits of botanical connections and horticultural therapy experiences directly to them.

FAVORITE FLOWER. Kaifa has too many favorites to pick one quickly. But if pressed, she will name amaranth (despite its often-aggressive reseeding) because of its incredible design diversity. She enjoys the dichotomy of both its whimsy and stately aesthetics, along with the texture defining its beauty, including both the softer and jewel tone color palettes.

WHIT MCCLURE

Floral Designer

LOS ANGELES, CALIFORNIA

WHIT HAZEN

Whit Hazen is a floral design studio specializing in artful and whimsical floral installations and styling services for corporate and private events, weddings, editorials, and film and television. Founder Whit McClure is also known for "Petals and Politics," her photography series that uses flowers to spell out messages of racial and gender equity, abolition, and social justice.

Whit collaborated with Counter Culture Coffee to celebrate the release of a seasonal coffee called "Perennial." This arrangement is part of a set of floral postcards with a coffee-stained patina that Whit Hazen paired with a bag of coffee and a bouquet to raise proceeds for Summaeverythang Community Center, a nonprofit devoted to Black and Brown empowerment, activities that included providing free organic produce boxes to recipients in South Central Los Angeles.

WHIT MCCLURE'S STORY is one of inspiration, integrity, and authenticity. As a studio-based designer who established Whit Hazen in 2016, she is known for creating whimsical, bold, and seasonally-inspired floral arrangements and installations that merge her passions for art, flowers, and politics.

Constantly inspired by nature's abundant beauty and driven to respect and protect its resources, Whit says her aesthetic is also influenced by color, form, graphic design, and architecture. "I create beauty while at the same time I express my strong opinions, using my voice and resources to speak truth to power. My hope is that my artwork encourages others to also pursue more of this in their lives."

Whit's "Petals and Politics" series, which she began in 2018, is one of the most visible ways she expresses her values. Compelled to speak out about issues and causes she believes in, Whit's vignettes read like floral slogans: "No More Jails", "Say Her Name", and "Remember Your Power" are among the messages. "Rather than

"This awareness inspired me to look into how seasonality impacted the flower world and our access to blooms. I realized something so beautiful was also quite political."

losing people on social media, I think I gained more followers. I think it's important for us as entrepreneurs to recognize we're not working in a bubble. The things happening in our communities, for better or for worse, are going to have an impact on our businesses."

Her studio name, Whit Hazen, comes from family roots. "'Hazen' is my mom's first name. She goes by her middle name, but I think Hazen is really rad and that it should be out there, so I combined our two names: Whit and Hazen. As my business keeps growing, and as I want to do design projects beyond flowers, I know I can carry on with Whit Hazen."

Childhood summers spent with her grandparents in Birmingham, Alabama,

were an important influence, Whit says. "My dad's parents were both educators who became avid gardeners in their retirement. I spent summer breaks going to museums, most notably civil rights museums and landmarks, as well as shopping at plant nurseries and garden centers. At the time, I was just going where they took me, but in hindsight, I see how those experiences made a lasting impression on what I now see as my purpose in working with flowers as a means to create a beautiful and just world."

Whit's interest in nature deepened while attending the University of Louisville, where she studied sociology. During a spring break trip to North Carolina, she was introduced to community gardening as a way of community organizing and combating food insecurity. After graduating in 2009, Whit continued to focus on opportunities where she could learn more about growing food. She took a job working on a blueberry farm in Maine, and while she found the work rewarding in many ways, she also felt isolated as a Black queer woman in a rural environment. She decided it was important to her to work more closely with marginalized communities in cities. When the blueberry farm job ended, she relocated to Washington, DC, where her sister lived. "DC turned out to be an incredible place for me to be," she says. "The movement to bring more access to healthy food was taking shape, and I began working for nonprofits that were building gardens within marginalized communities in the city."

The demands of the nonprofit industry eventually drained Whit and she shifted gears to become an entrepreneur and work for herself. As co-owner of a dog walking collective, Whit found herself outdoors nearly as much as when she was gardening or farming. "I walked by the same yards every day and couldn't help but

notice flowers and their seasons," she recalls. "This awareness inspired me to look into how seasonality impacted the flower world and our access to blooms. I realized something so beautiful was also quite political. I also realized working with flowers could be a way for me to merge my creativity with my love for bringing people together."

She began creating bouquets for her own home, discovering locally grown flowers at DC's farmers' markets and freelancing for a local florist for special events. The more flowers became a part of her life, the more Whit embraced them as her artistic medium.

In 2015, feeling ready for a shift, Whit relocated to new soil. A good friend in Los Angeles convinced her the city would be a great place to unleash her creative spirit. Whit used the change in scenery as an opportunity to dive fully into the floral industry, immersing herself in and taking full advantage of Southern California's year-round botanical abundance.

ABOVE
"Petals and Politics" is Whit's ongoing floral activism series featuring her designs, which she then photographs to telegraph messages about causes and issues, such as this one: "Say Her Name," in honor of Breonna Taylor. "I encourage people to hang one up as a daily reminder about how we must recommit ourselves to justice each and every day."

"Remember Your Power" is one of Whit's most popular pieces in the series. "In a year when so many things outside of ourselves have felt out of our control, this reminder of the personal power we each hold, and can tap into at any time, has the ability to positively shift and change both ourselves and the world around us," she wrote on her Instagram feed. "It is timely and needed."

"I want to serve as a 'possibility model' for fellow Black and queer people seeking to be successful as creatives in a field where they don't see many others like themselves."

In addition to designing for weddings and events, Whit Hazen offers custom floral bouquets for delivery in the greater Los Angeles area. Her online shop includes artfully-composed "Designer's Choice" arrangements, which feature the season's most beautiful blooms.

Her studio also provides interior floral styling for fellow small businesses in her community and works with brands and companies for gifting arrangements and events, as well as with publications for editorial styling. The breadth of Whit's work also extended into Hollywood, where she was the floral stylist for season two of Showtime's *The L Word: Generation Q.*

"I have built a fulfilling community here with other florists and I would say my arrangements addressing political issues is probably the biggest thing making my work stand out," she says. "I want to serve as a 'possibility model' for fellow Black and queer people seeking to be successful as creatives in a field where they don't see many others like themselves."

FAVORITE FLOWER. "My favorite flowers change by the season, but if I had to choose, I would name dahlias and passionflowers as my favorites."

OPPOSITE
"Peony Perfection," stands apart as a vivid Whit Hazen bouquet designed for local planner Heartthrob Weddings.

AISHAH & SEBASTIAN LURRY

Flower Farmers

CAIRO, GEORGIA

FOR THE LOVE OF BOTANICALS

Aishah Lurry navigated her floral beginnings in the picturesque town of Patagonia, Arizona. Growing for farmers' markets and floral pop-ups became not just a passion, but her business. She fell in love with Sebastian and had the opportunity to relocate to family land in Cairo, Georgia.

"I want people to know my business is rooted in joy. Sebastian and I wanted to take something we love and share it. Flowers are beautiful but also serve such a practical environmental function. We feel lucky to be stewards of our garden on ancestral land."

For the Love of Botanicals offers a vibrant
and colorful selection of cut flowers
for the DIY bouquet enthusiast, as well
as other items to uplift the spirit.

GROWING, DESIGNING, AND SELLING artisan cut flowers in Patagonia, Arizona, seems a world (and several garden zones) away from her childhood in Boston, but as Aishah Lurry reflects on her journey, the strong throughlines of art, plants, and community are evident. With a mother who is an artist and a childhood home in a renovated piano factory, Aishah was exposed to creative surroundings at an early age.

To nurture the curiosity of her seven-year-old child, Aishah's mother gave her a few seeds to plant in the community garden. These seeds—for radishes, carrots, and tomatoes—inspired a lifelong love of gardening, Aishah recalls. "I remember harvesting and sharing the bounty from my little garden plot with my friends as we played outdoors. It was a magical experience." As an adult, in search of sunshine and warmer temperatures, Aishah relocated to the Desert Southwest in 2008. She landed in Patagonia (population 1000), a town located less than twenty miles from the US-Mexico border that was developed as a trading and supply center for nearby mines and

ranches in the mid-nineteenth century. By the time Aishah and her husband Sebastian Lurry settled there, the tiny town had become a destination for artists and tourists.

She began working as the sprout-house manager at The Tree of Life Center, reconnecting with gardening and plants. When the center closed in 2017, Aishah knew she wanted to make a creative change and establish her own flower farm.

"Whatever happened, my goal was to become 'unbossed,'" she explains. "I knew I would be much happier working for myself."

As she spread the word about her floral endeavor, the opportunity to sell her bouquets at nearby farmers' markets became a reality. Aishah tapped into her prior experience as a personal trainer, which led to one of her fitness clients offering her a space to sell bouquets at the health-food store she managed.

Aishah wanted to learn more and enrolled in an online flower-farming

course. "Creating a vision board helped me develop a plan about what I wanted my business to look like. I noticed few African Americans in the world of floriculture at that time," she says, "and I decided I would love to inspire others to join this industry. Growing flowers is one of the most organic things any African American can do."

"We all live in accordance with the cycle of life. Things live and they die. Then we must move on. Gardening teaches us this. It is a life lesson I have learned well."

Through Patagonia Flower Farm, Aishah enjoyed spreading her philosophy about how "enjoying cut flowers directly affects our mental health." Georgia's moderate growing conditions, compared to the arid Midwest, encouraged Aishah to shift her perspective and embrace their new forever home. Growing in a different zone offers new opportunities to explore, experiment, and expand. Adapting to a new growing season, Aishah looks forward to growing and designing arrangements that can feature

OPPOSITE
Dahlias are always wanted—by brides and everyday floral-enthusiasts. The blooms are full and add panache to any arrangement.

a broader palette of plant material, including bulbs, ornamental shrubs, and garden roses.

For the Love of Botanicals offers specialty cut flowers, allowing their customers to create beautiful bouquets during the high season. As they grow, Aishah and Sebastian have plans for a space to offer botanical treasures like kokedama, terrarium plants, and botanical-inspired apparel. They hope that their farm will evolve into a sanctuary of botanical art and inspiration, a place where the love for all things green and growing is celebrated.

"My husband and I see the value of flower farming and how beneficial it is to expand on offering flowers all year-round. When I am asked how I have successfully grown blooms in the past, I merely answer—I put my seeds in the ground and ask the ancestors for guidance." The ancestors have led this dynamic couple to Cairo, Georgia, where there is room to grow and bloom and expand their operation. Together, Aishah and Sebastian want to encourage other people of color to not just grow flowers as a profession, but to consider the benefits of connecting with the earth using botanicals.

FAVORITE FLOWER. Sky-blue statice is most significant to Aishah, due to its unusual color. (Almost all other statice varieties are purple.) "While difficult to germinate, the clear blue color stands out in any arrangement, whether fresh or dried," she says. "Anyone seeing the ethereal color is sure to be as enchanted as I am."

LEFT
For the Love of Botanicals also forces
the bulbs of spring for all to enjoy.

RIGHT
The climate in Cairo, Georgia, will be perfect for
growing Lisianthus in the field. The rains of Georgia
will allow For the Love of Botanicals to grow an
assortment of unique flowers for arrangements.

TALIA BOONE

Flower Entrepreneur

LOS ANGELES, CALIFORNIA

POSTAL PETALS

Talia Boone is the founder and CEO of Los Angeles-based Postal Petals, an online floral start-up. She wants to revolutionize the way people experience flowers by identifying floral design as a therapeutic and creative exercise. Postal Petals manifests the values of a conscious, ethical, and inclusive brand by making intentional choices about how the company is run and where it sources flowers.

IF YOU SCANNED an imaginary dictionary for a definition of "bouquet of social justice," it's certain there would be a photograph of Talia Boone holding an open box of cut flowers. Yet, as an experienced marketing strategist, her relationship with flowers began as a personal rather than as a professional outlet.

Talia's Los Angeles-based agency INTER:SECT brings socially strategic consulting services to clients in sports, entertainment, business, and technology. In 2020, during the early days of the pandemic, Talia's therapist suggested she return to her favorite go-to self-care activity of arranging flowers to relieve the anxiety she was experiencing around life's uncertainties.

After not being able to access high-quality, fresh-cut flowers to arrange at home because the Los Angeles Flower Market closed in spring 2020 due to area lockdowns, Talia hunted to find a company who instead could ship flowers directly to her home. She found a flower wholesaler suppling large volumes of flowers to clients around

the world and reached out intending to convince him to reduce his minimums and ship her a box of blooms to play with at her home.

The two spoke for more than two hours, and what Talia learned about flower sourcing inspired her concept for Postal Petals. By the end of July 2020, just a few months after her first conversation with the wholesaler, Talia's new venture was in beta format with nearly twenty farm partners signed up to ship orders. By September 2020, Postal Petals was open for business.

Talia's concept for her business is simple. She partners with flower farms to ship boxes of fresh-cut bundles of flowers for customers to create DIY arrangements at home. Postal Petals fills a need to provide flowers to consumers eager for a connection to nature, which has been especially valuable during the pandemic. In addition, Talia wanted her business to support domestic floral agriculture, a segment also impacted by the pandemic. In the farms, located near her in California and elsewhere around the US, she has

It only took one experience holding stems in her hands for her to fall in love with the activity, something she found peaceful and a healthy relief from work stress.

found an openness to new market opportunities. "I'm constantly in awe this concept was devised in the mind of someone who simply loves arranging flowers, that it happened during a pandemic, and that it's now steadily growing, bloom by bloom," she observes. "I'm humbled at what it's become and excited about the possibilities of where it will continue to grow."

She knows when you care about people and the issues impacting their daily lives, it's nearly impossible for these same issues not to affect you on a personal level. In what would become an antidote to her concerns, Talia was first introduced to flower arranging several years ago by a friend. It only took one experience holding stems in her hands for her to fall in love with the activity, something she found peaceful and a healthy relief from work stress. Her first bouquet was simple: blush-colored

roses. Since then, Talia has made floral arranging part of her regular routine.

Postal Petals encourages DIY flower arranging as a form of creative expression and curates floral-design workshops called "Petal Riots" for consumer and corporate clientele. Leaning into the wellness benefits of floral activations, Talia encourages engagement with flowers holistically. With ongoing market research, Postal Petals will continue to reflect Talia's core values, as well as dedication to social justice.

FAVORITE FLOWER. Talia's favorite flower is the calla lily, a blossom she has loved since she was a little girl. Regal and statuesque with long stems and shapely blooms, Talia also appreciates how easy it is to design with calla lilies. "You can casually drop a few stems into a vase and the resulting arrangement looks exquisite," she says.

EPILOGUE

Myriah Towner

PRESERVING OUR HERITAGE; NURTURING OUR LEGACY. As you have read in the previous chapters, each and every single one of the flower farmers and florists who grace these pages has expressed brilliant creativity, flourishing entrepreneurship, and a deep and strong desire to bring joy and healing to their communities through blooms and bouquets of natural beauty. You can find Black joy in each of their stories, and I love the way flowers are a constant and central part of their work.

I started working as a freelance floral designer in the summer of 2018, when I met New York-based florists Molly Culver of Molly Oliver Flowers and Sylvia Lukach of Cape Lily Flowers. I was inspired, delighted, and comforted by the beauty of flowers, and knew then my hands had to work with flowers, but I had never done so professionally and had no idea where to begin. I also hardly ever saw people

who looked like me pursuing floristry or flower farming. While there are still very few of us represented in the industry, I am so inspired by the powerful stories of the Black flower farmers and florists in this book, who all have such a deep connection to and a larger motivation for floristry work. I think of how long Urban Buds's Mimo Davis has been growing cut flowers and how much knowledge she has to share, and then I think of budding flower farmers like Sunbird Flowers's Whitney Jaye (about whom I contributed a profile to this book) who is learning from elders around her how best to carry on the legacy of floral work today and how to inspire Black flower farmers in the future.

As background, I come from a family of farmers. My maternal grandparents worked the fields, picking cotton in East Texas, and my grandfather was a farmer. My uncle, Jimi, still today carries on our

"Black farmers—through resilience, endurance, determination, and creation of opportunities of financial and cultural independence—have continuously played a critical role in the economic and agricultural growth of the United States."

family's legacy of farming in rural Texas, a job he has held now for more than forty years. It was not until I was older and did a short stint as a farm-based educator and volunteer farmer when I really started connecting with him and his work as a farmer. Over the last few years, we have had several important conversations about his legacy: Where will all his farming knowledge go when his time on this earth comes to an end?

From these conversations, I realized there was a real issue at hand: no one is documenting and preserving the legacy of Black farmers in this country. Therefore, I have felt compelled to do my part in preserving this incredible knowledge in the best way I know how—through storytelling. As founder of Black Farmer Stories, my work is to preserve the knowledge, cultural heritage, and legacy of Black farmers by telling their stories. I aim to capture

the heart of resilience and joy embodied in so much of their work. By documenting the stories of Black farmers, my hope is to connect Black people to our ancestral histories and our relationship to land. I hope and trust sharing these stories will inspire people, help increase support and resources for Black farmers, and ultimately elevate their voices and demonstrate the vital role they hold in this country.

As my Uncle Jimi says, "There's a lot of Black farmers in this country, but you don't hear much about them." He hopes the next generation of Black farmers will return to the land and carry on the legacy of his and others' work, and I deeply hope so, too.

Ashley Pellerin, a dear friend and advocate for Black farmers in Texas, once told me, "We stand to lose a wealth of knowledge and important history if we do not collect the stories of our Black elders and those of the younger generation who are making the choice to continue to farm." This work is not only important. It is critical. Despite a history of systematic oppression, Black farmers—through resilience, endurance, determination, and creation of opportunities of financial and cultural independence—have continuously played a critical role in the economic and agricultural growth of the United States, as well as in the liberation and sustainability of Black communities. Through farming, Black farmers have made incredible advancements to improve their own families' livelihoods along with the livelihoods of their communities.

Even with these significant contributions to America's success, Black farmers, to this day, continue to be subjected to racial discrimination, a fact resulting in the horrific theft and loss of millions of acres of Black-owned land. To quantify and underscore this tragic history, Black farmers owned 15 million acres of land in 1920, a number decreased today to just about 1 million acres. This is a tremendous and urgent public crisis still needing to be addressed. The words of Black farmer champion Ralph Paige—as quoted in a 1992 article in *The New York Times*—still ring true: "This isn't just another Black farmer going out of business, it is our community losing a piece of the country."

The harm is doubled as we consider what is at risk if we also lose the stories of sacrifice, the tales of resilience, and the personal anecdotes of creating to survive, in addition to the loss of land. It's particularly vital to tell these stories of Black flower farmers and florists at a time when so much of the history of our people has already been erased.

It is precisely this intergenerational exchange of knowledge, the act of passing down knowledge from one generation to the next, that I am personally committed to in my own work. I know this activity is also vital for sustaining and preserving our work in these industries, particularly in agriculture. As each generation passes, we stand the risk of losing the history, knowledge, and legacy of these Black flower farmers—stories such as those shared in this book's earlier pages—that have been and still are so crucial to this country's legacy.

Thank you to all the Black farmers, florists, and land stewards who continue to cultivate and care for the land and bring joy to us through flowers. Your hands, your creative minds, and your determination are an inspiration.

RESOURCES

You are encouraged to support the individuals featured in *Black Flora* when you make your floral purchases. In this section, we've also collected recommended resources from our contributors and from the creatives profiled in *Black Flora*. From publications to organizations, here are their suggestions to further connect you with BIPOC farming and floral design resources. This is a dynamic list and one we'll be continuously updating at blackflorabook.com. Please feel welcome to forward any additional suggestions to: info@blackflorabook.com.

SOCIALS.

Ashley Robinson
12amsunshine.com
@12amsunshine

Gina Lett Shrewsbury
inspirationsbygina.com
@inspirationsbygina

Shanda Zelaya
flordecasadesigns.com
@flordecasa_designs

Kristen Griffith-Vanderyacht
wildbloomfloral.com
@kristengvy

Hermon Black
hbfiori.com
@hbfiori_hermonb

The Wild Mother
thewildmother.com
@thewildmother

Mimo Davis
urbanbudscitygrownflowers.com
@urbanbuds

Bron-Zuri Hansboro
theflowerguybron.com
@theflowerguybron

Drew Rios
rogueandfoxfloral.com
@rogueandfox

Joy Proctor
joyproctor.com
@joyproctor

Dee Hall
mermaidcityflowers.com
@mermaidcityflowers

Nicole Cordier
@cordier.botanical.art

Hannah Morgan
fortunateorchard.com
@fortunate_orchard

Natasha Graham
yosemiteflowerfarm.com
@yosemiteflowerfarm

Isha Foss
ishafossevents.com
@ishafoss
@lynnhavenflorist

Whitney Jaye
sunbirdflowers.com
@sunbirdflowers

RESOURCES

Kiara Hancock
khancockevents.com
@k.hancock

Taj & Victoria Cotten
perry-winklefarm.com
@cotten_picked

Kaifa Anderson-Hall
plantsandbloomsreimagined.org
@bloomin318

Whit McClure
whithazen.com
@whit_hazen

Aishah & Sebastian Lurry
patagoniaflowerfarm.com
@patagoniaflowerfarm

Talia Boone
postalpetals.com
@postalpetals

ALSO BY THE AUTHOR.

The Urban Garden: 101 Ways to Grow Food and Beauty in the City by Teresa J. Speight and Kathy Jentz. Cool Springs Press (March 2022)

OTHER PUBLICATIONS.

Farming While Black: Soul Fire Farm's Practical Guide to Liberation on the Land by Leah Penniman. Chelsea Green Publishing (October 2018)

Freedom Farmers: Agricultural Resistance and the Black Freedom Movement by Monica M. White. University of North Carolina Press (January 2019)

We Are Each Other's Harvest by Natalie Baszile. Amistad (April 2021)

DIRECTORIES & WEBSITES.

Mayesh.com "Black-Owned Floral Design Businesses" (blog.mayesh.com/black-owned-floral-design-businesses)

Postal Petals, "Black Florists" (postal-petals.myshopify.com/pages/black-florists)

ORGANIZATIONS & GROUPS.

Black Farmers Collective,
blackfarmerscollective.com,
@blackfarmerscollective

Black Farmer Fund,
blackfarmerfund.org,
@blackfarmerfund

Black Farmer Stories,
blackfarmerstories.com,
@blackfarmerstories

Black Flower Farmers,
@blackflowerfarmers

Black Girl Florists,
blackgirlflorists.com,
@blackgirlflorists

Ethos West Collective,
ethoswestcollective.com,
@ethoswestcollective

The National Society of Black Wedding
& Event Professionals,
nsbwep.com, @nsbwep

Northeast Farmers of Color Land Trust,
nefoclandtrust.org,
@NEFOCLandTrust

NOTABLE PROJECTS.

Anne Spencer House and Garden
Museum, annespencermuseum.com

Black Botanists Week,
blackbotanistsweek.weebly.com,
@blackbotanistsweek

Black Sanctuary Gardens,
pinehouseediblegardens.com/
black-sanctuary-gardens,
@blksanctuarygardens

Florists of Color, @floristsofcolor

PHOTO CREDITS

Page 3: Lauren Crew, with floral styling by Whit McClure

Page 7: Audrey Gallagher

Pages 11, 207: Isaiah D. Woolfolk, Founder and Visual Creative, Legac Virginia

Page 14: Teri Speight

Pages 16–17, 194–195, 205 (bottom): Dawn M. Trimble

Page 19: Nate King

Pages 20–25: Ashley Robinson

Pages 26–29: Bloom Photography

Page 30: Annie Hall Photography

Page 32: (top) GunnShot Photography, (bottom) Robin Jolin Photography

Page 33: (top) Courtesy of Gina Lett Shrewsberry; (bottom, left) Christine Glebov Photography

Pages 33 (bottom, right), 34: CHLOE JACKMAN PHOTOGRAPHY

Page 35: Sarah Fischback

Page 37: Emily Gude

Page 38: Kyla Jeanette Photography

Page 42: Courtesy of the Big Flower Fight/Netflix

Pages 44–49: Kristen Griffith-VanderYacht

Page 51: Gertie Gebre

Page 54: Tori Del Photography

Page 56: Rachel Maucieri Visuals

Pages 58–60, 64 (bottom): The Wild Mother

Page 64 (top): Robyn Icks Photography

Pages 67, 72–73: Carmen Troesser

Pages 68–70: Urban Buds

Page 75: Tiffany Marie Buckley

Page 76: Clear Sky Images

Page 79: M Harris Studio

Page 80: Lindsay Mears Studio

Page 83: D Clearview Photography

Pages 85, 87, 91: Nate Jensen

Pages 86 and 88 (bottom): Patrick Le

Page 88 (top): Rougue & Fox Floral Co.

Page 92: Kurt Boomer

Pages 94, 97 (bottom), 99 (left): Jose Villa

Pages 95, 99 (right): Joy Proctor

Page 96: Elizabeth Messina

Pages 97 (top), 100: Greg Finck

Pages 103–104: Sarah Bartley of Lumiere Creative Co.

Page 107: Kate Thompson Photography

Page 108: Anna Pacheco & Sarah Anderson

Page 110: Heather Stadler

Pages 112–113: Alicia Greenwell

Page 115: Heather Stadler

Pages 117–118: Jenny Jimenez

Pages 119–121: Fortunate Orchards

Page 122: Jessica Wood Photography

Pages 124–129: Niesha Blancas

Page 131: Eleise Thever Photography

Pages 133, 139: David Abel

Page 134: Justin Hankins

Pages 135–138: Eleise Theuer Photography

Pages 140–144: Kiyah C

Page 147: Ericka Kreutz

Page 148: James Moes

Page 149: Kiara Hancock

Page 151: (top, left) J. Anne Photography; (top, right) James Moes; (bottom, right) Lauren Kendall

Pages 151 (bottom, left), 154: Sarah Falugo

Pages 152–153: Sarah Carpenter Weddings

Page 156: Anna-Rhesa Versola

Pages 158–163: Taij & Victoria Cotten

Pages 165–167: Kaifa Anderson-Hall

PHOTO CREDITS

ABOUT THE AUTHOR

TERESA J. SPEIGHT is the Urban Garden and Container Garden Chair, District 1, for National Garden Clubs, Inc., and the founder and president of the Jabali Amani Garden Collective, a garden club for Minority women who enjoy gardening. Through her blog and podcast, *Cottage in the Court*, she offers a unique perspective on connecting with the earth, as well as curated garden experiences for small groups. Teri also offers one-on-one garden coaching, specializing in earth-friendly practices. She is the co-author of *The Urban Garden*.

ABRA LEE is an Atlanta-based horticulturist, author, and speaker. Abra's career milestones include serving as the arborist for the City of Atlanta; managing the landscapes for Hartsfield-Jackson Atlanta International Airport and George Bush Intercontinental Airport in Houston; and member in the Longwood Gardens Society of Fellows, a global network of public horticulture professionals. Her career now focuses on researching and writing about Black American garden history and she is the author of the forthcoming Timber Press book, *Conquer the Soil: Black America and the Untold Stories of Our Country's Gardeners, Farmers, and Growers*. Learn more at conquerthesoil.com.

MYRIAH TOWER is the founder of Black Farmer Stories, a digital platform and multimedia project that preserves the history, legacy, and agricultural knowledge of Black farmers and ranchers in the US through storytelling, and increases the knowledge of the general public about these important histories and stories. Learn more at blackfarmerstories.com.

DAWN M. TRIMBLE is an Atlanta artist who creates original works rooted within the various narratives of human vulnerability. Intuitively drawing from her passion and background in interior design and architecture, she explores the elements of light, space, and composition through her use of color and texture. Initially drawn to the medium of watercolor because of its transparency, she is a graduate of Auburn University's College of Architecture, Design & Construction (interior design) and Georgia Tech's School of Architecture (architecture). Learn more at dawnmtrimbleart.com.